EXPOSING SPIRITUALITY IN HEALTHCARE

DR. MICHAEL W. ELMORE

ISBN
978-1-959314-76-9 (Paperback)
978-1-959314-77-6 (eBook)
978-1-959314-75-2 (Hardcover)

To my loving and devoted wife

Coleen Elmore

For nearly 45 years of marriage she has loved, encouraged, and supported me in every endeavor of my life. With all my love.

"All our dreams can come true, if we have the courage to pursue them."

-Walt Disney

TABLE OF CONTENTS

ACKNOWLEDGEMENTS

The author wants to thank the following people for their support throughout writing this book. A special word of thanks goes to Ellen Maze for the constant encouragement that she extended to me. Through chance meeting, she has given me many ideas for promoting, editing and publishing this book. She has also become a good friend.

Thanks go to Lori Boruff, president of the Aledo Christian Writer's Group. Lori has provided encouragement, information about publishing, and facilitates a warm and caring writing group that I belong to. I am grateful for our relationship.

Of course, a big round of thanks goes to Rebecca Faust and the design team at *Quantum Discovery* for making this book possible.

Finally yet importantly, my wife Coleen Elmore who helped edit page after page of writing providing suggestions all along the way. She has offered untold love and unfailing support. A warm thanks to everyone.

FOREWORD

Before my first novel went to print, I was introduced to a fascinating and gregarious personality on Facebook who was busily finishing up his first book; the one you hold in your hand. Although my novel is fiction and deals with the paranormal in a made-up world, Michael and I found an instant kinship because his book deals with the paranormal breaking into our real world right under our noses. Being as we are both Believers in the One true God, we endeavored to encourage and exhort one another in the business of sharing our God-given vision to the world. Now that he has completed his book and given me the honor of reading it, I must say… my friend Michael is on to something.

How many times have you taken your child to the doctor, hoping to get the straight medical scoop on the problem, only to receive pseudo-scientific irreligious gibberish in its place? Every Believer has faced this predicament at one time or another; be it visiting the physician for yourself, a grandma, a child or a sick friend. All we ask is to be treated with the best science available and then sent home to have those we *trust* to pray to the One true God on our behalf. What we do *not* ask is to be drawn into the medical practitioners' other-worldly and/or pagan belief system and treated with methods that our Bible specifically warns us to avoid.

God abhors sorcery. He detests the practices of the pagan priests. The ways of the foreigner he finds abominable. These facts are established throughout the Books of Moses; Genesis through Deuteronomy. You think they are out of date? Think again. God does not change (Malachi 3:6), so you can count on Him and His word 100%. So the question remains, what does author Michael Elmore offer us with this extremely well-researched and thought-out book? Michael offers *awareness of the wiles of the enemy.*

Beware, lest you be deceived. Isn't that what we all want to avoid? Deception? Michael has collected for you dozens of pagan practices that have slithered into the medical profession and oftentimes seamlessly melded into the popular culture. We should not be surprised at this. The enemy can and will use any avenue available to draw the children of God away from His protection and even His salvation.

Dear Patient: take heed. Read this book and have your eyes opened. I know mine were from the first chapter. Read this terrific non-fiction tome and you will no longer accept your doctor's word at face value once he begins to delve into the occult in prescribing your treatment.

Dear Christian Medical Practitioner: be forewarned. You will be surprised to learn that many if not all of the bizarre, touchy-feely methods those nurses are teaching you (and certifying you in) are actually ancient non-biblical practices that your God finds abominable.

We all make choices in this life, and God makes it pretty simple. Choose Him, and you choose life (Deuteronomy 30:19). Choose the other way… you get the idea.

God bless you,

Ellen C. Maze
Author,

Rabbit: Chasing Beth Rider, Rabbit Legacy,
Rabbit Redemption, Rabbit Anomaly, Londundrum
The Corsescu Chronicles: The Judging, Damascus Road,
Tree of Life, Anathema, Nouns

PREFACE

This book celebrates the medical profession. Doctors, nurses, CNA's, HHA's, chaplains and all other disciplines are valued and appreciated by the author. As a chaplain, he has seen firsthand, the incredible work these people do. It is the intent of this book to highlight the importance of their work in the medical field, something which none of us can do without. All of us should be grateful for their compassion, hard work and tireless dedication.

More and more medical professionals are aware of some of the touch therapies discussed in this book. However, most have no idea about the spiritual connections that lie just beneath the surface of these practices. Even Christians who work in the medical field will be surprised and even shocked to learn how touch therapies and other forms of alternative medicine contradict their faith in Christ. Awareness of this fact may cause Christian medical professionals to re-think how their faith can co-exist in this type of environment or even if it can co-exist at all. These are difficult choices.

Another thing that readers need to be aware of is that this book is written for Christians. It makes no apology for this. It is written for Christian medical professionals, hospital and hospice chaplains, pastors and teachers, Christian college and seminary professors as well as every believer that may potentially face important medical decisions regarding alternative care.

Christian nurses are particularly targeted as a niche that this book is dedicated to. There are 2.9 million nurses in the U.S. Of these, 1,480,000 claim to be Christian. Since alternative therapies target nurses because of their patient access, it is only fair that this book offers nurses a message of hope and help in Christ Jesus. Know this, that wherever you are, you are not alone. Not only are there a multitude of other Christian professionals being confronted with the same issues, but you also have the promise of Christ who left us the legacy that *"I will never leave you nor forsake you"* (Hebrews 13:5). He said, *"I will be with you until the end of the age"* (Matthew 28:20).

Dr. Michael W. Elmore
Urbana, Illinois 2022

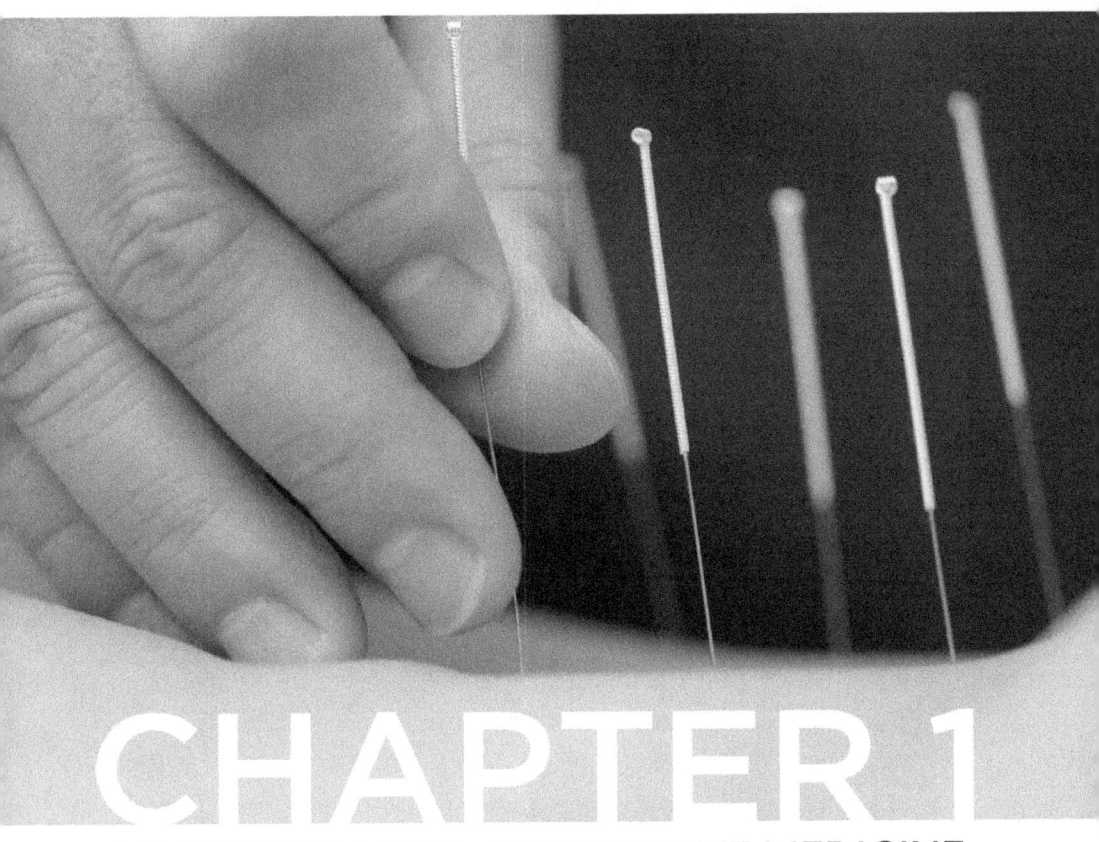

CHAPTER 1
MAINSTREAMING ALTERNATIVE MEDICINE

CHAPTER 1
MAINSTREAMING ALTERNATIVE MEDICINE

*"Do not bite at the bait of pleasure, till you know
there is no hook beneath it."*
— *Thomas Jefferson*

Health Care is the number one topic on the hearts and minds of Americans everywhere from the President of the United States, Congress and each member of our society. Health Care is experiencing changes at an extraordinary rate. The wheels are in motion for the greatest transformation in this country's health system since the advent of social programs like Medicare and Medicaid. Reforms in health care are catapulting their way through Congress. Initiatives will change medicine in a sweeping manner in an effort to fix a broken system. Whether you support these changes or not health care is experiencing a revolution.

Health care is transforming as medical technology and innovation constantly updates itself daily. Advances in medicine are taking place so rapidly, and procedures that were theory as recently as five years ago, are now part of mainstream medical care. Laparoscopic surgery has changed the course of expected outcomes, shortened hospital stays and reduced the estimates for recuperation by several weeks.

Health care insurance is changing as well. Innovations such as group coverage, Preferred Provider Organizations, and Health Maintenance Organizations are now the norm. Physician discounts, co-pays, deductibles, and coverage limits are an everyday concern for Americans. Medical costs are inflating at a skyrocketing rate. The costs are increasing because of expensive new medical technology and high pharmaceutical prices. Creating physician groups, merging of health care organizations, a focus on generic medications and shortening hospital stays are all attempts to cope with health care's spiraling costs.

Into this environment of changing health care, a new field of medicine has arisen. This field promises to cut costs, provide more effective care and focus on the whole person, body, mind and spirit. This care is attractive to health care administrators whose concern is for the "bottom line". Unlike the scientifically based medical model that centers on drug therapy and surgical interventions, it offers modalities that are less invasive and based on a paradigm of spirituality. Into the confusing, ever-changing face of health care, a new modality is introducing therapies called Alternative Medicine.

THE DEVELOPMENT OF ALTERNATIVE MEDICINE

Alternative medicine is ambiguous in nature and difficult to define. Some forms of alternative care, which once were outside the sphere of conventional medicine, are now accepted practice. This blurring and blending of therapeutic choices has made it more difficult to make a distinction between scientific models and alternative practices. In short, alternative medicine is making it into mainstream health care.

In Western culture, the term alternative medicine has come to mean "any healing practice outside of conventional medicine". Early studies indicate that alternative medicine is not as effective as its conventional counterparts are. It also, encompasses therapies that are part of Eastern culture and religious practices.

It is important to understand exactly what alternative medicine is. Alternative medicine is part of two divisions of treatment: *alternative medicine and complementary medicine.* Both terms are interchangeable. The Mayo Clinic of Rochester, Minnesota refers to alternative care as *Integrative Alternative Therapies.* According to the Mayo Clinic, alternative therapies refer to "unconventional treatments that are used *instead of* traditional medical care". *Complementary Alternative Therapies* refer to treatments that augment traditional medical therapies.[1]

According to the National Center for Complementary Medicine, 1800 types of alternative therapies have been categorized. NCCAM is one of 27 government agencies that make up the National Institutes of Health. Its role is to explore complementary and alternative healing practices in the context of scientific training, complementary and alternative medical research, and disseminate authoritative information to the public and professionals. Its mission is fourfold. NCCAM focuses on:

- **Research** - support clinical and basic science research projects in CAM by awarding grants across the country and around the world. They design, study, and analyze clinical and laboratory-based studies on the NIH campus in Bethesda, Maryland.
- **Research training and career development** - awards grants that provide training and career development opportunities for pre-doctoral, post-doctoral, and career researchers.
- **Outreach** - sponsors conferences, educational programs, and exhibits; operates a clearinghouse to answer inquiries and requests for information; provides a Web site and printed publications; and holds town meetings at selected locations in the United States.
- **Integration** - integrates scientifically proven CAM practices into conventional medicine. Announces published research results and studies ways to integrate evidence-based CAM practices into conventional medical care. They also support programs to develop models for incorporating CAM into the curriculum of medical, dental, and nursing schools.

One classification that NCCAM endorses is "touch therapies". This book seeks to explore three of these therapies. Besides these, some of the more popular therapies include massage, acupuncture and acupressure, reflexology, Shiatsu, Heller Work, Rolfing, Chinese massage and Kinesiology.

Of the hundreds of alternative therapies that NCCAM recognizes, some of them build on practices that pre-date our time by as much as 5,000 years. A number of these come from cultural environments outside of the

---

[1]   Bauer, Brent M. D. (2002). *Alternative Medicine and Your Health*. Rochester, MN: Mayo Clinic Health Information. p.2

Western paradigm and its focus on the Scientific Method. For example, Traditional Chinese Medicine is part of the philosophic concept of balance between yin and yang, Qi, body fluids, emotion and spirit, as well as Taoist philosophy and Chinese culture that is as old as antiquity. It encompasses a belief system foreign to Christianity as revealed in Scripture. Traditional Chinese Medicine is responsible for the development of acupuncture, herbalism, and certain diet and exercise regimens.

> *"Many alternative therapies encompass a belief system foreign to Christianity as revealed in Scripture".*

Ayurveda (science of life), is a medical method dating back 2,500 years, with roots in the Vedic school of Hinduism and Indian culture. It incorporates holistic practices that were popularized by the influx of Indian immigrants following the Second World War. One school of Ayurveda is from the tradition of "bonesetting" and is responsible for developing osteopathy and chiropractics in the United States.[2]

A number of alternative therapies are Western in origin and come from Christian religious traditions. They are an inherent part of God-given gifts and abilities. Examples of these are music therapy, art therapy and animal therapy. Hospitals and hospices across the country employ harpists, buy or borrow artwork that soothes and calms agitated patients, or offers the companionship and love that only a dog can provide.

One therapist shares his story. "My name is Gary Malkin. I am a seven-time Emmy and ASCAP award-winning composer. I shifted the focus of my work from being a Hollywood composer to creating music-infused resources that focus on integrative health care applications. I created a technique that I have called 'Audio Alchemy'. This contemplative listening modality provides an accelerated way to cultivate greater emotional and spiritual intelligence.

Another way to describe these intelligences relates to the propensity for a person to be more circumspect and less reactive during the dramatic 'bottlenecks' of our lives. These often accelerate overt or covert fears, which can tend to compromise people's capacity to be resilient, or even to be

---

[2]   Evidence-based Research in Complementary and Alternative Medicine https://www.hindawi.com/journals/ecam/2005/472791/ (Accessed October 14, 2022).

self-healing. This occurs due to the psychoneuroimmunilogical challenges to the immune system.

As a composer, I learned to create and articulate these things. They are a result of my dedication to creating a work that was released 8 years ago, entitled, *Graceful Passages: A Companion for Living and Dying*. Along with this, I wrote another piece released 5 years ago, called *Care for the Journey: Music and Messages for Sustaining the Heart of Healthcare*. *Graceful Passages* is an 'iconic' work in the field of Hospice, Palliative Care, and Cancer Care, specifically as a spiritual support tool.

These music infused resources, are "potent forms of non-pharmacological interventions for the alleviation of fears around illness and the end of life process. They also serve as resources for strengthening and addressing burnout for the healthcare professional." Healthcare professionals around the world use these resources, often instead of pharmaceuticals, to address spiritual and emotional suffering.

Because of the phenomenal responses from *Graceful Passages*, we have learned how music-infused wisdom can help people deal with serious levels of spiritual and emotional suffering. These can profoundly influence the healing processes of patients, families and their caregivers. We have learned that customized music, along with intimate contact, as featured in *Graceful Passages,* can provide a powerful form of spiritual healing. This kind of healing is simply not found, offered, or addressed in the current healthcare system".[3]

Of course, not all alternative therapies available in our society and health care marketplace today are intrinsic to the gifts and capacities that God has given. Many originate in religious practices and cultural forms based on Eastern mysticism and religion. One business that advertises the use of these Eastern forms of therapy is *The Dragontree Holistic Day Spa* in Portland, Oregon. At their recent grand opening, the Dragontree issued this statement in their press release: "About The Dragontree Holistic Day Spa: Portland's finest day spa offers a variety of services to still the mind and mend the body. The Dragontree is the perfect place to receive massage, facials, acupuncture, waxing, Ayurvedic counseling, and herbal consultations. You may also gather with friends and family and receive foot treatments, head, neck, and shoulder massages, and hand treatments. All

---

[3]   Malkin, Gary. *Wisdom of the World, Inc, Media for a Meaningful Life.*

treatments fit each individual's specific needs with the intention of creating the space for true healing to occur".[4]

THE GROWTH OF ALTERNATIVE MEDICINE

The use of alternative therapies is growing astronomically. In the United States alone, an ever-increasing number of medical colleges that are offering courses in alternative medicine. As of this writing, three separate research surveys found that 729 schools, 125 medical schools offering an M.D. degree and 25 medical colleges offering a Doctor of Osteopathy degree have courses in alternative medicine. Similar to this, 585 nursing programs, that is 60% of nursing schools, 95 % of osteopathic colleges and 84.4% of nursing programs teach some form of alternative medicine. The University Of Arizona College Of Medicine offers a program in Integrative Medicine under the leadership of Dr. Andrew Weil. Accredited Naturopathic colleges and universities are increasing in popularity across the U.S. and Canada. In Connecticut, the University of Connecticut Medical School sponsors Ayurveda seminars and courses.

There is a virtual explosion in the use of alternative medicine taking place today. Carefully kept statistical tables bear this out. Nurse Education Specialist, Donna Bingenheimer, R.N. of Shore Memorial Hospital in Somers Point, New Jersey submits the following statistics to corroborate this growth. She writes, "Statistics compiled by the National Institute of Health (NIH) as recently as 2008 found that 38% of adults, 4 in 10, and 12% of children, 1 in 9, are using some form of Complementary and Alternative Medicine. The delivery of patient centered care obligates healthcare providers to know, understand, recognize and support patient choices about their care related to complementary and integrative therapies. Hospitals are offering touch therapies such as reflexology, Reiki and gentle massage to help with relaxation, pain management, and symptom relief.[5]

Why is there such a growth in alternative and complementary therapies? Some believe that it is for several reasons. There is a low-level of

---

[4]   Invite Spirit to Join You https://thedragontree.com/2022/10/28/invite-spirit-to-join-you/ (Accessed October 14, 2022)

[5]   Bingenheimer, Donna RN. Shore Memorial Hospital, Somers Point New Jersey.

scientific understanding in a large segment of the population. In addition, there is an increasing anti-scientific bias, as well as a growing interest in New Age ideas. There are also rigorous marketing campaigns facilitated by the alternative medical community aimed at consumers. Another reason for the growth of alternative therapies is an increase in conspiracy theories toward conventional medicine and pharmaceutical companies. A growing number of people have no access to public or private health insurance, which leads them to looking for lower out-of-pocket costs through other avenues. Occasionally, even medical doctors are marketing alternative medicine to make up for the loss of income because of insurance discounting and the promise of other sources of revenue.

"Most alternative medicine used was in place of standard medical treatments".

A study published in 1998 indicates that most alternative medicine used was in place of standard medical treatments. Approximately 34.4 percent of those studied used alternative medicine *as a replacement for conventional care*. The research found that those who used alternative medicine have a higher education level or report poorer health status. Dissatisfaction with conventional treatments was not a meaningful factor in the choice. Instead, the majority of alternative medicine users appear to be doing so because "they find these health care alternatives to be more congruent with their own values, beliefs, and philosophy." In particular, subjects reported a holistic orientation to health, and a transformational experience that changed their worldview. A number of groups look favorably upon environmentalism, feminism, psychology, and spirituality and personal growth. They may also suffer from a variety of common and minor ailments -- notably anxiety, back problems, and chronic pain.

To what degree is alternative medicine part of treatment in the United States? A 2002 survey of U.S. adults 18 years and older conducted by the National Center for Disease Control (CDC) and the National Center for Complementary and Alternative Medicine indicates:

- 74.6% had used some form of complementary and alternative medicine.
- 62.1% had done so within the preceding twelve months.

- When prayer for health reasons is not part of this, these figures fell to 49.8% and 36.0%, respectively.
- 45.2% had in the last twelve months used prayer for health reasons, either through praying for their own health or through others praying for them.
- 54.9% used CAM along with conventional medicine.
- 14.8% sought care from a licensed or certified practitioner, suggesting, most individuals who use CAM prefer to treat themselves.
- Most people used CAM to treat or prevent musculoskeletal conditions or other conditions associated with chronic or recurring pain.
- Women were more likely than men to use CAM. The largest sex difference is in the use of mind-body therapies.
- Except for the groups of therapies that included prayer, the use of CAM increased as education levels increased.
- The most common CAM therapies used in the U.S. in 2002 were prayer (45.2%), herbalism (18.9%), breathing exercises (11.6%), meditation (7.6%), chiropractic medicine (7.5%), yoga (5.1%), body work (5.0%), diet-based therapy (3.5%), progressive relaxation (3.0%), mega-vitamin therapy (2.8%) and visualization (2.1%).
- In 2004, a survey of nearly 1,400 U.S. hospitals found that more than one in four (25%) offered alternative and complementary therapies such as acupuncture, homeopathy, and massage therapy.[6]

In one survey conducted by the Center for Disease Control, researcher Robert Velarde, M. D. reports that people are using alternative and complementary therapies for various reasons. Fifty percent said they thought alternative medicine "would be interesting to try." Others are dissatisfied with conventional health care for various reasons, such as the bureaucratic mess and rising costs. Some have lost confidence because of the lack of solutions offered by conventional medicine for chronic conditions, such as arthritis, fatigue, cancer, and AIDS. Still another group is disappointed that conventional medicine primarily offers only two options: drug therapy

---

[6] Complementary and alternative medicine use among adults https://www.sciencedirect.com/science/article/abs/pii/S1543115004000389 (Accessed November 8, 2022).

and surgery. In a world where "natural" remedies seem more effective than conventional remedies, these options seem reasonable.

Alternative health-care practitioners have the reputation of spending more time with patients than conventional doctors do. They view patients as whole persons, and in many instances offer "just the right thing" for the condition in question.[7]

According to one statistical analysis, we find that the most common reasons that people give for seeking integrative medical care are as follows:

- 54.9% of people thought that combining complementary alternative medicine with conventional medicine would help.
- 50.1% thought it would be interesting to try.
- 27.7% thought conventional medicine would not help.
- 25.8% thought conventional medicine professionals were uninformed.
- 13.2% thought that conventional medicine was just too expensive.[8]

This trend in the use of integrative alternative care is growing. More people, for a variety of reasons, are turning to alternative therapies for medical care. The most recent government funded survey found that 36% of adults interviewed reported using some form of complementary or alternative medicine. That number rises to 62% when use of the mega vitamins and prayer are included.

Interestingly, this survey also reports that women are more likely to use complementary and alternative therapies than men are. It also notes the most common condition that people turn to alternative medicine is for back pain. Over all, the number one reason people give for using a complementary therapy is that they want to try something in addition to conventional treatments because conventional treatment have left them dissatisfied. These trends are increasing. In the latest report, about $36 billion-$47 billion was spent last year on complementary and alternative therapies.

---

[7]   Alternative Medicine, Apologetics, and the Church http://equip.org/articles/alternative-medicine-apologetics-and –the-church (Accessed October 15, 2022).

[8]   Bauer, Brent M.D., (2007). *Book of Alternative Medicine.* New York, New York: Time Inc. pp. 14, 15

The trend in hospital care continues to escalate as well. Currently, 25% of all hospitals and well over that number of hospices offer a variety of alternative choices to their patients and families.

"Currently, 25% of all hospitals offer alternative choices".

Sue Warner, an administrator at Courage Center for Rehabilitation in Minneapolis, Minnesota serves as an illustration of this trend in the use of alternative therapies in her institution. "Courage Center is a Minneapolis-based rehabilitation center that's been around since 1928. We are incorporating mind-body techniques in our traditional therapies (PT, OT, and Speech). Matthew Sanford, a yoga instructor who is also a paraplegic, leads the effort. We have taught three groups of therapists the mind-body techniques to use with clients. What we have learned is that this training, besides benefiting our clients, is helping with staff morale and retention.

In addition to this innovative approach, we also offer Watsu (water shiatsu), Ai Chi, and Reiki, massage, a yoga class, Tai Chi, fully accessible fitness centers and warm water pools in our Minneapolis and Stillwater facilities".[9]

In summary, we must recognize that integrative medicine refers to combining complementary and alternative therapies with conventional medicine. Statistics show that this trend in care is growing because this is what people want.[10]

THE INEFFECTIVENESS OF ALTERNATIVE MEDICINE

Some scientists reject the use of alternative medicine because according to them, "there is only medicine that has been tested and medicine that has not. There is medicine that works and medicine that may not work." These scientists advocate a classification based on scientific evidence, and state that, "alternative medicine, in our view, has not been scientifically tested and its advocates deny the need for such testing." The U.S. Institute of

---

[9]　Warner, Sue. Administrator, *Courage Center Rehabilitation Center*, Minneapolis, MN 2009.

[10]　Bauer, Brent M.D. 2007. *Book of Alternative Medicine.* New York, New York: Time Inc. pp. 10, 11

Medicine analyzed this approach in defining alternative care, which it called normative. They found that alternative medicine is problematic because some is tested, but much of it lacks strong evidence. The IOM found that in a study of 160 systematic reviews of alternative medical techniques, 20% were ineffective and 21% had insufficient evidence. These studies also found that results for the efficacy of CAM was 38.4% and concluded a positive outcome in only 12.4% of cases. 4.8% showed no affect, 0.69% concluded harmful effect, and 56.6% concluded there was insufficient evidence.

Well-known proponent of evidence-based medicine, Edzard Ernst, Professor of Complementary Medicine at the University of Exeter, uses the term alternative medicine, but agrees that all treatments, whether "mainstream" or "alternative", ought to hold to standards of the scientific method. Ernst characterizes the evidence for many alternative techniques as weak, nonexistent, or negative.[11]

Other members of the health care community agree with Ernst and make statements regarding the ineffectiveness of alternative therapies despite the claims made by its advocates. One study suggests that because alternative techniques lack evidence, some propose defining it as non-evidence based medicine or not medicine at all. These researchers suggest the evidence-based approach to defining CAM is problematic. Because some CAM lacks research, it suggests that it lacks the evidence required by mainline medical techniques. The consensus of many studies concludes that medicine is not medicine if it lacks verifiable scientific proof.

THE EFFECTIVENESS OF PRAYER AS ALTERNATIVE THERAPY

Interestingly, the most effective alternative therapy of those used in any study is prayer. The following studies make the case in point. Out of 191 randomized controlled studies of healing, 124 demonstrate significant effects that exceed a probability of 0.05% or better. Until recently, medical journals routinely rejected studies and articles on healing, and most healing studies were only available in parapsychology journals. Fortunately, this is

---

[11]   Trick or Treatment? Alternative Medicine on Trial https://www.ncbi.nlm.nih.gov/pmc/articles/PMC2553546/ (Accessed November 8, 2022).

changing. In the past dozen years, some of the most impressive studies are part of respected medical journals.

For example, Randolph C. Byrd 1988, explored intercessory prayer in a coronary care unit. The experimental group received prayer sent by Christians praying many miles from the hospital. The prayer group scored significantly lower than the control group on a scale for severity of problems devised by Byrd. Significantly, fewer patients in the prayer group needed intubation, ventilation or antibiotics, had cardiopulmonary arrests, developed pneumonia, or were dependent on diuretics.

William Harris 1999, repeated Byrd's study in another randomized, controlled, double-blind, parallel group trial of 990 consecutively admitted patients on the CCU. There were 466 in the prayer group and 524 in the control group. The prayer group showed significantly more improvement than the control group.

In 1998, Fred Seeker arranged a randomized, double-blind trial of distant healing on 40 volunteers who had AIDS. At six months following the initial assessment, the prayer group had significantly fewer AIDS related illnesses and lower severity of illness. Visits to doctors were less frequent, as were hospitalizations, and days in the hospital. These are three of the best healing studies available. It is also of note that they are part of the record in respected, conventional medical journals.[12]

Christians should remember that genuine healing is the prerogative of God and that intercessory prayer invites the Holy Spirit to work his grace and make healing possible. As James 5:13, 14 states, *"The effectual fervent prayer of a righteous man avails much"*.

CATEGORIES OF ALTERNATIVE MEDICINE

Alternative medicine is classified into five major categories: whole medical systems, mind-body techniques, biologically based therapies, manipulative therapies, body-based therapies, and energy therapies. Within these categories, we will identify the major alternatives.

---

[12]   Shannon, Scott. (2001). *Handbook of Complementary and Alternative Therapies in Mental Health.* San Diego, CA: Academic Press. pp. 258, 259.

Biologically Based Therapies

Herbal Medicine

Herbalism is the oldest known form of health care, using plants and plant extracts to treat disease and promote wellness. Either an herb or a variety of herbs forms the treating substance. Chinese herbal mixtures also can contain minerals and animal parts. Conventional drug therapy extracts a single active chemical agent, while herbal medicine usually makes use of the medicinal plant in its whole form.

Orthomolecular Medicine

Orthomolecular medicine uses combinations of vitamins, minerals, and amino acids found in the body to treat specific conditions and to maintain health. Nutrition comes in diagnosis and treatment. Sometimes referred to as nutritional medicine, orthomolecular therapy emphasizes supplementing the diet with high-dose combinations of vitamins, minerals, enzymes, hormones (such as melatonin), and amino acids. Dosages often far exceed the amounts normally consumed in the diet.

Chelation Therapy

In this therapy, a drug binds with and removes excess of toxic amounts of metals or minerals (such as lead, copper, iron, or calcium) from the bloodstream. In conventional Western medicine, Chelation therapy is a widely accepted way to treat lead poisoning and other heavy metal poisoning. Copper Chelation has been under investigation as a cancer treatment. Chelation therapy with ethylenediaminetetraacetic acid (EDTA) is a alternative medicine therapy used to remove calcium and treat atherosclerosis. The effectiveness and safety of this therapy are under evaluation scientifically. Side effects can be serious or sometimes fatal.

Energy Therapies

Energy therapies focus on the energy fields thought to exist in and around the body (bio-fields). They encompass the use of external energy sources (electromagnetic fields) to influence health and healing. All energy therapies contain a core belief of the existence of a universal life force or subtle energy that resides in and around the body. Energy therapies include magnets, Reiki, Therapeutic Touch, yoga, Ayurveda, acupuncture, and qi gong. Practitioners of energy therapies typically place their hands on or near the body and use their energy to influence the energy field of the person.

> *"All energy therapies contain a core belief of the existence of a universal life force."*

Magnets

Magnet-based therapies use static magnetic fields, pulsed electrical fields, and alternating current or direct current fields. Magnets, in particular, have become a popular treatment for various musculoskeletal conditions. Static magnet therapy remains scientifically unproven, especially for pain relief, which is one of the most common applications. Research studies of the effectiveness of static magnets have been inconclusive.

Reiki

Reiki is a technique of Japanese origin in which practitioners channel energy through their hands and transfer it into the person's body to promote healing. Practitioners complete a course of training with the intention of developing the ability to direct healing energy to others. Practioner's do not touch the client or they make very light contact with their fingertips. Its effectiveness is questionable.

Therapeutic Touch

Therapeutic Touch, sometimes referred to as the "laying on of hands", uses the therapist's healing energy to identify and repair imbalances in a person's bio-field. Unlike Reiki, therapists do not touch the person. Instead, therapists move their hands back and forth over them. Therapeutic Touch helps reduce anxiety and improves a sense of well-being in people who have cancer, but rigorous studies are not available to show other effects. Therapeutic Touch has gained acceptance by many holistic nurses who integrate it into their hospital work routine.

Manipulation Therapies

Manipulative and body-based therapies treat various conditions through manipulation. These therapies include chiropractic, massage, reflexology, and postural reeducation.

Chiropractics

In chiropractics, the relationship between the structure of the spine and the function of the nervous system is key to maintaining or restoring health. The main method for correcting this relationship is spinal manipulation. Chiropractors also may provide physical therapies such as heat and cold, electric stimulation, rehabilitation strategies, massage, acupressure or recommend exercises and lifestyle changes. Chiropractics is actively studied, although its effectiveness is not clear at this time.

Massage Therapy

Massage therapy is the manipulation of body tissues to promote wellness and reduce pain and stress. It involves a variety of light-touch and deep-touch techniques. It uses stroking and kneading (as used in Swedish massage), applying pressure to specific points. It is used in Shiatsu, acupressure, and neuromuscular massage. Massage therapists claim to help the musculoskeletal, nervous, and circulatory systems of the body. Other healing affects of massage include the benefits of caring human touch, basic needs that are unmet in the lives of many people.

Reflexology

In reflexology, manual pressure connects to specific areas of the foot that practitioners believe correspond to different organs or systems of the body. Stimulation of these areas assists in removing the blockage of energy responsible for pain or disease in the corresponding body part. Reflexology may help relieve anxiety in people who have cancer.

Mind-Body Therapies

Mind-body techniques work on the theory that mental and emotional factors can influence physical health. Behavioral, psychologic, social, and spiritual methods can preserve health and prevent or cure disease. Methods include meditation, relaxation techniques, guided imagery, hypnotherapy (hypnosis), and biofeedback.

Meditation

In meditation, people center their attention or systematically focus on particular aspects of inner or outer experience. Meditation usually involves sitting or resting quietly with the eyes closed. Sometimes it involves the repetitive sounding of a phrase (a *mantra*) meant to help the person focus.

> *"Most meditation practices are within a religious or spiritual context."*

The most studied forms of meditation are "transcendental meditation" and "mindfulness meditation". Most meditation practices are within a religious or spiritual context. Their ultimate goal is spiritual growth, personal transformation, and transcendental experience.

Relaxation Techniques

Relaxation techniques are practices specifically designed to relieve tension and strain. The specific technique aims at reducing the activity of the nerves that control the stress response (sympathetic nervous system), lowering blood pressure, easing muscle tension, slowing metabolic processes, or altering brain waves. Relaxation techniques succeed in combination with other techniques as well.

Guided Imagery

Guided imagery involves the use of mental images to promote relaxation and wellness, reduce pain, and promote healing of a particular ailment such as cancer or psychogenic trauma. The images can involve any of the senses and is self-directed or guided by a practitioner, sometimes in a group setting. For example, a person with cancer imagines an army of white blood cells fighting against the cancer cells. Guided imagery lacks thorough scientific study.

Hypnotherapy

This alternative therapy arises from Western practice. In hypnotherapy (hypnosis), individuals move into an advanced state of relaxation and heightened attention. Hypnotized people become absorbed in the images suggested by the hypnotherapist and are able to suspend disbelief. Because of their focus, individuals are more open to suggestion. Hypnotherapy reports to help people change their behavior and improve their health. The mechanism of hypnotherapy remains invalidated from a scientific standpoint.

Biofeedback

Biofeedback is a method of bringing subconscious biologic processes under conscious control. Biofeedback involves the use of electronic devices to measure and report to the conscious mind information about physical processes such as heart rate, blood pressure, muscle tension, and the brain's electrical activity. With the help of a therapist or with training, people can understand why these functions change and can learn how to regulate them.

Whole Body Systems

Whole body systems are complete systems of diagnosis and practice. Several whole body medical systems exist, including Traditional Chinese Medicine, Ayurveda, and other unconventional Western practices of natural healing.

Traditional Chinese Medicine

Originating in China more than 2,000 years ago, this system bases itself on the idea that illness results from the improper flow of the life force *qi* (pronounced "chee"), through the body. Therapy balances the opposing forces of *yin* and *yang*, which manifest as heat and cold, external and internal, and deficiency or excess. Various practices preserve and restore qi and thus health. These include, diet, medicinal herbs, massage, a meditative exercise called *qi gong*, and acupuncture. One problem with traditional Chinese medicine is that standardization and quality control are almost nonexistent.

Acupuncture

Acupuncture is a therapy within Traditional Chinese Medicine. It is one of the most widely accepted alternative techniques in the Western world. Acupuncture involves stimulating *marma* (energy) points on the body, usually by inserting very fine needles into the skin and underlying tissues. Stimulating these specific points unblocks the flow of *qi* along energy pathways or *meridians* (there are more than 350 marma points along the meridians) and thus restores balance between yin and yang. Stimulating acupuncture points through pressure is called acupressure.

Ayurveda

Ayurveda is the traditional medical system of Hinduism, found in India, originating more than 4,000 years ago. Ayurveda is the theory that illness is the result of imbalance in the body's universal life force or *prana*. Balancing this life force occurs by re-establishing the equilibrium of four bodily qualities called *doshas, vata, pitta,* and *kapha*.

Practitioners evaluate people by questioning them about symptoms, behavior, and lifestyle. They also evaluate the patient's overall appearance, including the eyes, tongue, and skin, and by taking their pulse and checking their urine and stool. Ayurveda uses diet, herbs, massage, meditation, yoga, and cleansing of the colon to restore balance within the body and with nature. Few well-designed studies of Ayurvedic practice are available.[13]

> *"Medical studies offer inconclusive evidence regarding their actual benefits".*

These therapies represent the most popular alternative practices that people are using in their medical care. Most claim some degree of effectiveness or people would not pay practitioners for their efforts. However, medical studies offer inconclusive evidence regarding their actual benefits. All too often, the sense of relief lies strictly in the personal belief of the individual. At times, clients will say that they "strongly believe" in one of these therapies and continue to visit that therapist. However, other individuals

---

[13] Overview of Integrative, Complementary, and Alternative Medicine https://www.merckmanuals.com/home/special-subjects/integrative,-complementary,-and-alternative-medicine/overview-of-integrative,-complementary,-and-alternative-medicine. (Accessed October 14, 2022).

may try the same therapist and decry the whole experience as bunk. These individuals may not be far from the truth according to conventional medicine. Medically speaking, there is little evidence that indicates that alternative medicine offers any tangible benefit.

INSURANCE AND INTEGRATIVE THERAPIES

In 1992, the National Institute of Health established the Office of Alternative Medicine (OAM) under pressure from a Congress alarmed by the soaring costs of health care and the frustrating fact that so many ailments go uncured.

According to the *New England Journal of Medicine*, one third of the population of the United States consulted health-care providers other than conventional medical doctors, spending nearly $14 billion for their services in 1991. Three quarters of this was out-of-pocket. In 2007 dollars, this amount tripled.

In the intensifying search to find a solution to the high cost of medical care, complementary methods are becoming recognized because they have lower costs and claim to work. Insurance companies are reaching out to explore the field of mind and body healing to lower the expenses they incur as part of conventional treatments. Their goal is to provide both good and cost-effective care. Insurance companies may also be attempting to re-coop some of the dollars that consumers are spending on complementary medical choices.

In the past few years, several insurers have come to recognize that non-conventional treatments can save them money. For example, several sessions of chiropractic or acupuncture treatments for lower back pain are substantially less expensive than surgery for a herniated disk. Some insurers are even creating alternative care insurance packages for consumers. Mutual of Omaha, found their lifestyle-based, "healthy-heart program" to be an effective money-saving preventative care that is significantly less expensive than angio-grams, angioplasties and other invasive treatments. Mutual of Omaha likes the savings the healthy-heart program offers. They determined the cost of an angioplasty is $18,000 and heart bypass $40,000-$50,000. They assume that if the program can save the price of one of those procedures, it saves money in the end. As a result, of Mutual of Omaha's success, 15 other insurance companies are now supporting similar programs as a valuable alternative to bypass surgery.[14]

St. Paul Fire and Marine, offers medical professional liability coverage for complementary and alternative medical providers. The company is the first national carrier to offer comprehensive health care related to property, casualty, and professional liability insurance. They offer these to providers who practice acupuncture, art therapy, biofeedback, dance therapy, drama therapy, homeopathy, massage therapy, music therapy, naturopathy, polarity therapy, and reflexology. St. Paul's policies feature coverage for complementary and alternative treatments that allows agents to adjust coverage limits when premiums renew. This policy is available in 49 states and so far, about 35 states have approved the rate filings.

Some self-insured companies in the state of Washington, *Microsoft among them*, have voluntarily written generous coverage for alternative practices into their health plans. One alternative for Microsoft employees includes unlimited access to all varieties of chiropractors, naturopaths and Christian Science healers.

Dr. Popik of Cigna HealthCare reports, "Consumers want high-touch medicine." He also comments that, "Alternative medicine is gaining broader acceptance, and it's something to look at in the future."[15]

CHALLENGES FOR INTEGRATIVE ALTERNATIVE MEDICINE

There are still hurdles that those who practice alternative medicine have to surmount. In some states, the only alternative therapies covered by insurance are those that are part of a reimbursable treatment. These include such things as physical therapy, massage, or any treatments delivered by a licensed health care professional.

Another challenge for alternative medicine is the *law*. Each state creates its own laws governing health care practice. There may also be local laws that affect healthcare delivery, such as laws restricting the practice of acupuncture or massage. Many state legislatures have not caught up

---

[14]   Barnett, Libby. (1996). *Reiki Energy Medicine*. Rochester, Vermont: Healing Arts Press. p.94

[15]   Ibid.

with the current trend toward complementary and alternative therapies in health care.

Legislation is another area in which the promotion of alternative health care must continue to work. Diane Miller, of Minnesota, founded National Health Freedom Action to support grassroots organizers in multiple states. NHFA is a strong advocate for state jurisdiction of health care issues and works to protect the rights of the state in behalf of its citizens. They support broad-based consumer access to all health care options and work to protect the diversity within and among state healthcare cultures.

"Millions are embracing alternative care as never before".

CONCERNS ABOUT INTEGRATIVE ALTERNATIVE MEDICINE

There is no doubt that health care is uppermost in the hearts and minds of everyday Americans. The industry is constantly changing. Some of these changes are tsunami-like in nature. They will leave an enduring imprint on the way health care operates in this country.

Because of the exorbant costs of conventional medical treatment and procedures, the use of alternative therapies is growing at a phenomenal rate. While medical experts question the efficacy of complementary and alternative therapies, millions are embracing alternative care as never before. Joining them, are hospital administrations and health care insurers, all of which are trying to find a way to streamline and reduce costs. Low cost alternative care seems to be one answer that leads to the perfect solution.

Christians need to be wary of some forms of integrative alternative medicine and not sacrifice their faith in Christ on the altar of less expensive medical care. Philosophies inherent to alternative medicine do not always mesh with Christian teaching and belief. Many therapies are extensions of ancient religious practices based in Eastern philosophy and religion. Many are replete with practice and thought foreign to Christianity. Christians must be careful in embracing certain forms of complementary medicine as it contradicts the foundations of their faith.

STUDY QUESTIONS

MAINSTREAMING ALTERNATIVE MEDICINE?

1. Define alternative medicine?

2. What are the most common alternative therapies used in the U. S.?

3. What percentage of U. S. hospitals uses alternative therapies?

4. What are some reasons people give for using alternative medicine?

5. What was the Institute of Medicine's conclusion regarding the effectiveness of Alternative Medicine?

6. What do medical studies show is the most effective form of alternative medicine?

7. What are the categories of alternative medicine? Give examples of specific therapies.

8. Why are many insurance companies offering coverage for alternative care?

9. What concerns should Christians have regarding alternative medicine?

CHAPTER 2

BUDDHISM'S ABSENCE OF GOD

CHAPTER 2
BUDDHISM'S ABSENCE OF GOD

*"Frisbeetarianism is the belief that when you die,
your soul goes up on the roof and gets stuck."*
— George Carlin

In many respects, alternative medicine is not medicine at all, but is a system of healing based on the philosophical and religious precepts of Eastern religion. When we discuss Eastern religion, we take into consideration two of the largest religious systems in the world: Buddhism and Hinduism. Hinduism confines itself to the Indian subcontinent and its millions of adherents. In contrast, although Buddhism originated in India, it quickly spread to engulf the entire civilizations of the Asian world. Beginning in Tibet and Nepal, the massive wave of Buddhist beliefs flooded China, Japan, Korea and Southeast Asia. Along the way, it mixed with and absorbed many other belief systems and folk religions to form a syncretistic whole.

It is important to have a basic understanding of Buddhism when studying about integrative alternative medicine. As we will see throughout this book, Buddhism is the foundation for the practice of many alternative therapies. Only by understanding the religious roots of alternative medicine will one be able to recognize that many alternative therapies are not medical modalities at all, but are actually belief systems. To understand Buddha, is to understand his religious system and how it plays such a vital role in alternative medicine and touch therapies.

BUDDHA, THE ENLIGHTENED ONE

Buddhist scholars agree that a historically accurate picture of the Buddha's life is impossible to reconstruct. Narratives about his life appeared four hundred years after his death. Devotees have embellished the accounts of his life, actions, and words. Take, for instance, the following story of the Buddha's birth:

"The child comes forth from his mother while she is standing up and holding on to the branch of a sacred tree. The Buddha is free of any afterbirth and is immediately able to walk and talk. He takes seven steps in each of the cardinal directions and proclaims himself ruler of the universe". Despite exaggerations about Buddha, a rough outline of his life is available. One must continually bear in mind, however, that beyond archaeological evidence proving his historical existence, we know very little about the circumstances of his life.

Siddhartha Gautama, the son of King Suddhodana Gautama, a chieftain (raja) of the Shakya clan, grew up as part of a family living within the Kshatriya caste. Siddhartha, meaning, "he who has accomplished his objectives," was born around 563 B.C. His father reigned over Kapilavastu, a small district on the Indian slope of the Himalayas in a region sandwiched between India and Nepal.

Shortly after Siddhartha's birth, a hermit named Asita allegedly had a vision in which he saw the gods rejoicing at the birth of a supreme man. Siddhartha "was born for the welfare and bliss of the entire world." Asita subsequently traveled to Suddhodana royal court where he saw the child. The hermit allegedly prophesied the following:

"This Prince, if he remains in the palace, when grown up, will become a great King and subjugate the whole world. Nevertheless, if he abandons the court to embrace a religious life, he will become a Buddha, the savior of the world".

King Suddhodana, believing that contact with human misery would prompt Siddhartha to leave home in search of spiritual truth, immediately ordered his servants to shield the prince from all contact with evil and suffering. Siddhartha would be a prisoner of luxury. To distract Siddhartha from the cares of this world, King Suddhodana gave his son many possessions, including three palaces and 40,000 dancing girls.

Legend has it that when Siddhartha reached the age of sixteen, five hundred women emerged as prospective brides. Eventually he chose as his bride his cousin Yasodhara. According to one account, he won her hand by performing "twelve marvelous feats in the art of archery."

Siddhartha's life was unfolding as his father had planned until the young prince, out of either curiosity or inner discontent, eluded his royal attendants and ventured into the outside world. Over a succession of several days, he visited nearby Lumbini Park, where he made some disturbing observations.

First, he crossed paths with an old man, broken and bent by age. On the next day, Siddhartha saw a diseased person, possibly a leper. During his third excursion, the prince viewed a corpse. When he took another trip on day four, he met an ascetic (a monk who practices self-denial).

Siddhartha was never the same. He decided that life is nothing but an experience plagued by sorrow. Why is there so much suffering? How can men escape that which is an inescapable round of torment? Is there no end to pain and sorrow? To answer these and other questions, Siddhartha left home and began a spiritual quest for truth. Some say he left on the very night Yasodhara gave birth to their son, Rahula ("hindrance").

For about six years, young Gautama wandered about as a poor beggar, studying meditation and philosophy. His pilgrimage led him to two yogis (spiritual teachers). He made every attempt to follow their path of spirituality. He ate nothing but seeds and grass, gradually reducing his diet to only a single grain of rice each day. In one experiment, he ate only dung.

Then Gautama met and joined a company of five monks with whom he practiced various methods of asceticism. He lay on thorns, wore rough-textured clothing, and refused to sit, choosing instead to crouch on his heels. He gave up cleansing his body until the dirt was so thick that it would fall from him of its own weight. Gautama would hold his breath until it felt as though someone were forcing a heated sword through his skull. He even slept in a yard where vultures and scavengers were eating rotting human corpses.

Siddhartha hoped to reach an understanding of life through his self-denial, but failed. He did however, gain a realization neither asceticism (self-inflicted pain and discomfort), nor extravagant living (as he had experienced in the royal court) brought "truth" any nearer. There existed a better path — the Middle Way. A good illustration of this path is a stringed musical instrument. If the strings are too loose, they will not play. On the other hand, if they are too tight, they will break.

When Siddhartha demonstrated this realization by eating a normal meal in front of his fellow monks, they deserted him. Undaunted, Gautama headed for Gaya (a major city in the northeast of India). There, beneath a full moon in May, he spread a mat under a fig tree on the banks of the Meranjana River and assumed the "lotus" position (sitting in a modified cross-legged manner). He vowed to remain there until he understood life's mysteries. It was his thirty-fifth birthday.

After stilling his mind "like a hummingbird poised in mid-air," Siddhartha began meditating. Within several hours, he allegedly saw an infinite succession of deaths and births in an ever-flowing stream of life. In other words, he had a vision that supported the doctrine of reincarnation. This is a foundational teaching of the Brahman religion of which he was well acquainted. With his mind purified and cleansed, he directed it to the passing and rebirth of beings. With divine vision, he saw them passing away and reborn, low and high, in happy or miserable existences, according to their *karma* or acts of good or evil.

> *"He had become the "awakened one," the "enlightened one," the Buddha".*

Siddhartha continued meditating until he reached complete enlightenment. "I realized that for me rebirth is destroyed, the holy life is now lived, my job is done, and there is nothing after this." With his vision came an internal perception of how to obtain liberation from *samsara*, or the cycle of rebirths. The young prince had lost his ignorance about the nature of this world. He understood everything. He had become the "awakened one," the "enlightened one," the Buddha.

Two months later and nearly one hundred miles from where he had achieved enlightenment, the Buddha gave his first sermon. Near the holy city of Benares, in the Deer Park, he presented an address called the "Wheel Doctrine." It contained the *Four Noble Truths*, which would serve as the foundational teachings of Buddhism.

For more than forty years, the Buddha continued teaching all who would listen. Then, tragedy struck at Kusinara in the district of Gorakhpur. Chunda the blacksmith fed the Buddha either spoiled pig's flesh or poisoned mushrooms. The Buddha quickly fell ill with dysentery and died at the age of eighty.[16]

TEACHINGS OF BUDDHISM

Its Scriptures Dharma is an Indian term, which means conformity with the basic principles of existence within the universe. It is simply the law of life. Within Buddhism, the Dharma took on specific meaning and comprise the teachings of the Buddha.

After the death of the Buddha, his disciples convened their first council at Rajagrha, where they tried to organize his teachings within a system of doctrines. Oral traditions passed to future generations of Buddhist monks within their communities in India. Four centuries later, about 80 B.C., Buddhist scribes finally compiled the teachings of the Buddha on paper. These became the *Pali Canon*. The written collection of the Buddha's teachings are also part of the *Tripitaka* (the "three baskets"), because they contain rules for conduct, methods for spiritual attainment, and the ethics taught by the Buddha.

Non-Existence of the Soul Like many of his contemporaries, the Buddha protested against the aristocratic religion of his day because religion had one, become corrupt and tyrannical, and second because it was too refined and intellectual for the common people. His teachings were open to all who would listen, taught clearly, and made easy to understand.

Contrary to the prevailing Brahman doctrine, the Buddha recruited disciples from all castes. According to him, nirvana (deliverance from suffering) is accessible to everyone who strictly obeys the laws of a monastic life, despite their caste. His teachings were an enormous step forward in reforming the religious corruption of his day in Indian culture.

In addition to this, the Buddha argued against the philosophical speculations of the Brahman priests, who tried to join the concept of the soul's oneness with oneness in god (Brahman). He rejected subservience to a supreme God and denied belief in an eternal self. Some people misunderstand his ideas concerning *karma*. He believed that karma determines the rebirth a person experiences according to past merit. The

---

[16]   Martin, Walter. *Kingdom of the Cults*, Bethany House, Minneapolis, Minnesota, 2003 p. 312.

Buddha did not believe in the rebirth of the self or soul. Instead, he taught that at birth there is a re-emergence of a person's identity.

Buddhism's Concept of Heaven The Buddha defined *nirvana* differently from the Brahmins. Brahmanism taught that nirvana or *moksha* is within grasp when the individual soul becomes one with the Universal Soul. The Buddha held that nirvana is the end of rebirths — that the goal of *extinguishing the identity of an individual is certain.* In Hinduism, the individual self is like the raindrop that falls into the ocean, becoming one with the Universal Soul. In describing nirvana in Buddhism, the identity of a person is like a candle flame that is blown out.

The Buddha taught that true nirvana is not immediately accessible — several lives are necessary to achieve it. He declared that if nirvana depended only on suppressing all feeling and thought, then the deaf, the blind, and the insane could enter it. Instead, he said the journey to nirvana is long and difficult, but the fruits of this spiritual quest are inner peace and harmony with all beings and final deliverance from suffering.

View of Suffering The Buddha believed that suffering dominates the lives of all human beings, and he taught a practical way of deliverance from it. These teachings on suffering are the heart of the Dharma and the Four Noble Truths: (1) the universality of suffering (2) the origin of suffering (3) how to overcome suffering and (4) the way leading to suppressing suffering. The first Truth defines the nature of being, the second and third Truths develop various aspects of being, and the fourth Truth suggests a practical way to find deliverance from suffering, through reincarnation.[17]

By following the Fourth Noble Truths, a person supposedly will be able to eliminate selfish and false desires, the key to attaining nirvana. Those who reach complete "purity of thought and life" become an *arahat,* or someone who is "freed from the need of rebirth, ready for the peace of nirvana." Only those who distance themselves from all desire can attain this state.

These Truths enable the individual to experience detachment and by it, liberation from the cycle of rebirth. They are the key to empowering the individual to attain "Nothingness", or nirvana. The religious life is the

---

[17]   Walter Martin, *Kingdom of the Cults,* Bethany House, Minneapolis, Minnesota, 1997, p. 204 ff.

way out of the human dilemma of reincarnation. If followed, life on earth is a new dimension of Reality.

Salvation through Union with Nothingness Those who reach nirvana are free forever from all the anxieties, fears, and desires that possess ordinary people. They are free "from the eternal round of decay, suffering, and death." They will never again experience rebirth. Nirvana is a state of mind marked in this life by "a sense of liberation, inward peace and strength, insight into truth, the joy of complete oneness with reality, and love toward all creatures in the universe." After death, *there is total annihilation.*

Such a concept of nirvana is slightly different from the one embraced by the Brahmans of Siddhartha's day and by modern Hindus. Brahman Hinduism teaches that Enlightenment takes place when an individual soul unites with the Universal Soul. The Buddha, on the other hand, believed that extinguishing the soul requires that the individual's identity dissipate like smoke.

Karma, Salvation Though Good Works The second religious idea that distinguishes Buddhism from other religious ideas is notion of *karma.* A corollary to reincarnation, karma seeks to explain what factors determine the form a person is reborn in the next life. The Buddha stated that our good deeds and bad deeds accumulate either merit or debt, and the ratio of merit to debt determines the state of our next life. Rather than teaching the rebirth of the individual soul or "self", the Buddha maintained that only "karmic matter," or the elements that comprise a person's identity reincarnates. Even then, these elements rearrange at rebirth, "much as a 'chariot' is a name for a certain group of parts that can rearrange to be something else while still comprising the same parts."

> *"There is no personal 'soul' that continues to exist after someone dies".*

In other words, the Buddha taught that when someone is reborn, that they are not reborn at all. There is no personal "soul" that continues to exist after someone dies. What is reborn is nothing but rearranged karmic matter that was once a particular individual. The person, or the original "self" that once lived, no longer exists. Eventually, successive stages of karma, will extinguish the individual forever. This is the Buddhist idea of nirvana.

Unfortunately, becoming a Buddhist monk is the only way to reach nirvana from this present life. One must "abandon ordinary social living and join the monastic community, which Buddha built for those sincere in their quest for liberation." A person can reach nirvana only by leaving behind family, friends, and occupation, and joining a *sangha* (an alms-dependent order of Buddhist monks).

This does not mean the average person cannot follow the Buddha's teachings. However, according to the Buddha, they will not be able to attain nirvana in this lifetime. Nor will they benefit from the higher fruits of the dharma (such as inner tranquility). The best they can hope for is to be reborn as an individual who, in that next lifetime, will become a monk. According to the oldest Buddhist tradition, a woman will never reach nirvana from this life, even if she becomes a Buddhist nun. She must be reborn as a man who becomes a monk.

THE ABSENCE OF GOD

As a whole, Buddhism is a pantheistic religion that denies the existence of God in favor of *Nirvana*. Nirvana is a Universal Force of Life in which each person must one day join in union. In early Buddhism, the Buddha clearly states that "reliance and belief" in creation by a supreme being leads to lack of effort and inaction. This is a significant hindrance in the path to liberation in the Buddha's view. We should note the Buddha did not criticize veneration of the noble, veneration of the wise and learned, but only said the belief in the existence of a creator God fetters the mind to *samsara* or rebirth.

The Buddhist cannon records a conversation the Buddha had with a group of Hindu priests in his own words. "I approached the priests and contemplatives who hold that whatever a person experiences is all caused by a supreme being's act of creation. I spoke to them saying, 'Is it true that you hold that whatever a person experiences is all caused by a supreme being's act of creation?' Thus asked by me, they admitted, 'Yes.' Then I said to them,' in that case, a person is a killer of living beings because of a supreme being's act of creation. A person is a thief, unchaste, a liar, a divisive speaker, a harsh speaker, an idle chatterer, greedy, malicious, a holder of wrong views because of a supreme being's act of creation".

When one falls back on creation by a supreme being as being essential, monks, there is no desire, no effort [at the thought], this must or must not be done. This was my second righteous refutation of those priests and contemplatives who hold to such teachings, and such views."[18]

According to Buddha's own definition, Buddhists do not refer to the term "God" at all. The idea of a Supreme personal Being rests primarily in Christianity. In essence, Buddhism is pantheistic. Pantheism is the view that God is everything and everyone and that everyone and everything is God. Pantheism goes beyond polytheism to teach that everything is God. A tree is God, a rock is God, an animal is God, the sky is God, the sun is God, and together with these, you and I are God. Understanding pantheism is imperative to understanding the basis of touch therapies that rely heavily on the universal idea of an impersonal deity. This unknowable divinity manifests itself similarly to Buddhism. It is viewed as a universal energy force called Nirvana, and is comprised of all living things. This energy is ambiguous, all encompassing and inhabits space all around us. Buddhist calls this all-pervasive energy Nirvana, while the architects of touch therapies refer to it as the Universal Life Force.

THE EXISTENCE OF SPIRITS IN BUDDHISM

Although Buddhism denies the existence of God, it does have a strong belief in *devas* or spirits. Besides this, Buddhism teaches the existence of other Buddha's or "enlightened beings." According to Buddhism, devas are invisible to the physical human eye. Some humans can detect the presence of a deva. By opening themselves up to an extrasensory power, these individuals can see beings from other planes. Those who have cultivated a similar power of the ear can also hear their voices.

Most devas have the capacity to construct illusory forms which can be used to manifest themselves to the beings of lower worlds. Higher and lower devas are able to do this between one another. Devas do not need the same sustenance as humans do, although the lower kinds do eat and drink. The higher sorts of devas report to shine with their own intrinsic

18   Introducing Buddhism Fundamental Teachings https://www. thebuddhistsociety.org/page/fundamental-teachings (Accessed October 14, 2022)/

luminosity. Devas are capable of moving great distances speedily and of flying through the air. Lower devas sometimes do this through magical aids such as a flying chariot.

REGIONAL BUDDHISM AND SYNCRETISM

As Buddhism swept across China and the Asian continent, it encountered various religious practices of the peoples residing in those areas. Instead of abandoning the worship of provincial gods, spirits and ancestors, Buddhism and local religious beliefs merged to form syncretistic expressions of Buddhist practices.

The ancient Chinese religion of Taoism that pre-dates Buddhism by 2,500 years, focused on spirit and ancestral worship, magic, incantations and spells. In addition to Taoism, indigenous people groups worshipped local deities who they felt had influence over their daily lives. These individuals believed that certain peculiarly shaped rocks and boulders or old trees, as well as fields, streams and roads, possessed their own spirits. These superstitious beliefs continued from generation to generation. Even today, villagers and the less educated continue such worship.

"Buddhism and local religious beliefs merged to form syncretistic expressions of Buddhist practices".

Remember that even before the advent of Buddhism in China, there was already a large confluence of gods worshipped by the Chinese people. Many of these gods were heroes or anyone who had distinguished themselves by rendering meritorious services to the country. There were those who had helped to save the country from external aggression, or had helped to avert sufferings due to natural calamities. They became deities following death, and it is possible that some of these gods became a part of the country's mythos. One example is the *"Monkey god"* of the famous *"Journey to the West"*, whom the Chinese still pray to with great respect and solicit favors from in times of sickness and misfortune. Other gods or deities are patron saints of various professions. There is the god of Medicine and the patron saint of the Fishmongers. People view them with great respect and occasionally hold ceremonies hosted by trade associations to make offerings to them. Offerings include thanksgiving for successes earned in business or other professions and requests for continuing good fortune in the future is part of these festivals.

Vajrayana Buddhism — also known as Tibetan Buddhism, Tantric Buddhism, and Lamaism, is an element of the "diamond way". By implication, this means it is a precious, changeless, pure, and clear way. This offshoot of Buddhism developed during the fifth to sixth centuries A.D. as it spread through northern India, Nepal, and finally Tibet.

At that time, the prevailing belief of Tibet was the Bon religion, a mixture of shamanism, a form of witchcraft, magic, and primitive nature worship. Vajrayana grew up as a practice, with certain formulae designed to obtain magical powers. It also became part of Buddhism about A.D. 600-1200. Included in the Vajrayana tradition, are advanced meditative techniques: yoga, special hand gestures (*mudras*), spells, and chants. It also traces many of its doctrines from Vedantic and Tantric influences. Study of these texts details the use of clairvoyance, clairaudience, telepathy, and psychometry.

In the course of three centuries, Buddhism spread across the Asian continent and beyond. Its influence and syncretistic practices are pervasive to this day. Illustrating this is a 2004 newspaper article from Burma. The paper states, "Many Burmese and Thai Buddhists continue to worship spirits, while holding a strong belief in Buddhism's teaching on "karma". They realize that they have to go through a life cycle—birth, growing up, reaching adulthood, aging, the prospect of illness, death and reincarnation. They know too well that in passing each stage of life they will also experience hardships brought about by nature or circumstance, drought, famine, flooding, pestilence and unemployment. Rural peoples in both countries have devised folk explanations to make these events more understandable.

Of course, they realize that all things happen because of cause and effect, that man is responsible for his own actions. They believe in good and bad karma. At the same time, the power of the spirit world explains such events as unknown disease that takes the life of a family member, by a phenomenon of nature.

Beliefs in Buddhist teaching, respect good spirits and fear bad ones. These beliefs fuse together in the syncretistic practice of "folk Buddhism". Most place Buddhism higher than belief in the supernatural, even though most spirit worship predates it. People pray to Buddha before going to bed not only to ask for favors or to pay homage to the religion, but also to seek protection from malevolent spirits.[19]

SUMMARY OF BUDDHISM

It is important to have a thorough understanding of Buddhism and the tenets of its teachings. This enables us to understand the primitive roots in which touch therapies grow. Let us summarize the facts we have examined to make sure we clearly grasp them. First, Buddhism began about 2,500 years ago as a response to one man's reaction to the dilemma of poverty and suffering.

> *"Buddhism is a form of pantheism that underlies the belief that 'all is god and god is all.'"*

Second, although Buddhism is an offshoot of Hinduism, it adds unique components indigenous to its own belief system. The first of these is the idea of *nirvana*, or a universal energy force that consists of all things. In place of a personal, knowable God, Buddhism is a form of pantheism that underlies the belief that "all is god and god is all." It also promotes reincarnation, or a continuous cycle of rebirth and death. An individual may attain higher states of being in the next lifetime through practicing a system of good works called *karma*. Its goal is for the soul to merge with "nothingness" to escape the cycle of rebirth.

Buddhism experienced exponential growth through its first three centuries of existence. In essence, it devoured the eastern Asian continent. As it encountered other cultures and religions, it absorbed theses to form syncretistic regional variations that incorporated many indigenous practices. These practices include spirit and ancestral worship, the use of magic, divination, casting spells and incantations. Forms of this mixed influence in Buddhism exist to this present-day.

---

[19] Expansion of Buddhism into Southeast Asia https://en.unesco.org/silkroad/knowledge-bank/expansion-buddhism-southeast-asia (Accessed December 3, 2022).

WHY BUDDHISM IS IMPORTANT TO TOUCH THERAPIES AND ALTERNATIVE HEALTH CARE

A superficial glance will show that touch therapies, inexorably link to Buddhism and its practices. We will see the touch therapies explored in this book are part of Eastern antiquity. Touch therapies incorporate a belief system and practices similar to Buddhism, especially in its pantheistic concept of God and the existence of the Universal Life Force. Both Buddhism and touch medicine denounce the existence of a personal God and accept the idea that good works through karma and the cycle of rebirth replaces repentance, forgiveness and faith in Christ. Each uses clairvoyance, clairaudience and other forms of spirit contact forbidden in Scripture. Each is syncretistic, picking, choosing and merging whatever belief systems suit them best. Alternative medicine flagrantly mixes Eastern and Western philosophies, Christian and non-Christian ideas in the same breath to fulfill their purpose and reach their goals. As we begin to explore the touch therapies in this book, it will not take long before we will see that Buddhism significantly contributes to the exercise of touch therapies.

STUDY QUESTIONS
BUDDHISM'S ABSENCE OF GOD

1. Who is Buddha and what are the key elements of his life?

2. What is Pantheism?

3. What is the Buddhist concept of God?

4. What is Nirvana?

5. What is Karma?

6. What is Reincarnation?

7. What are devas?

8. How did the spread of Buddhism affect its teaching?

9. What is syncretism?

10. What kinds of occult practices are incorporated in Buddhism?

11. How does Christianity differ from Buddhism?

CHAPTER 3

HINDUISM'S SEARCH FOR
THE ONE TRUE GOD

CHAPTER 3
HINDUISM'S SEARCH FOR
THE ONE TRUE GOD

*"Ignorance is the night of the mind, but a night
without moon and star."*
— Confucius

In the West, Christianity is the crucial factor that led to the development of the modern health care system. This religious influence in health care began with the first community medical services offered at local monasteries in the Middle Ages. Eventually, it progressed to include the creation of denominational hospitals in the 19th Century. It is obvious that in the past few decades medicine is becoming more secularized and shedding most of its former religious ideology. Although some hospital's names continue to identify them with their former denominational affiliations, they no longer have any significant links to these religious institutions. The exceptions to this are Catholic hospitals, which retain their religious heritage and distinctives.

Because of this trend toward secularization, a new form of spirituality is creeping into our health systems. Because hospitals have shed the veneer of their former spiritual heritage, many have adopted a "generic" form of spirituality that attempts to honor all religious traditions. The days are gone when medical care grew out of the biblical concept of compassion motivated by the love of God in Christ. However, a new form of spirituality is filling the gap by implementing alternative therapies. What many people are unaware of is that alternative medicine has a religious basis just as conventional medicine did in Christianity. Alternative therapies historically align themselves with the cultural and philosophical soup of Eastern religions. Moreover, they are encroaching on our health care systems. Spiritual ideas foreign to Christianity and the values of conventional health care, like spiders, are weaving their way into the medical milieu.

In our previous chapter, we learned about the history, teachings and some of the strange spiritual exercises that are an inherent part of Buddhism. We also learned that it is imperative that we understand Buddhism's religious philosophy to recognize the spiritual underpinnings of alternative care. Just as we have seen that Buddhism plays an important role in integrative alternative therapies, we will discover that Hinduism also serves a vital role in developing alternative therapies as well. We must examine the history and religious past of Hinduism so we can better understand it connection with integrative care.

THE HISTORY AND DEVELOPMENT OF HINDUISM

The word Hindu comes from the river Indus. It simply means "the people who live near the Indus River" (in modern Pakistan). About 1,500 B.C. when the Aryans invaded India from the north, they brought their Indo-European sky gods with them. Later, as the two cultures mixed, it seems that their gods mixed too.

The earliest evidence for pre-historic religion in India dates back to the late Neolithic period (5500–2600 B.C.). The beliefs and practices of the pre-classical era (1,500–500 B.C.) is the source of the "historic Vedic religion". Modern Hinduism grew out of the Vedas, the oldest of which is the Rig-Veda, dating to 1,700–1,100 B.C. The Vedas center on the *worship of deities* such as *Indra*, *Varuna* and *Agni*, and on the *Soma* ritual. They performed fire-sacrifice, called *yajña*, and chanted Vedic mantras but did not build temples or icons. The oldest Vedic traditions exhibit strong similarities to Zoroastrianism and other Indo-European religions.

The major Sanskrit epics, *Ramayana* and *Mahabharata*, grew over a protracted period during the late centuries B.C. and the early centuries A.D. They contain mythological stories about the rulers and wars of ancient India. They also include religious and philosophical treatises. The later *Puranas* recount tales about *devas* and *devis*, their interactions with humans and their battles against *demons*.

Three major movements underpin a new epoch of Hindu thought: the advent and spread of Upanishadic, Jaina, and Buddhist philosophico-religious thought. Mahavira (24th Tirthankar of Jains) and Buddha (founder of Buddhism) taught that to achieve *moksha* or *nirvana*, one did not have to accept the authority of the Vedas or the caste system. Buddha went a step further and claimed the existence of the soul and God was unnecessary. Buddhism peaked during the reign of Asoka the Great of the Mauryan Empire, who unified the Indian subcontinent. In the 3rd century B.C., several schools of Hindu thought formally codified in Indian philosophy, including Samkhya, Yoga, Nyaya, Vaisheshika, Purva-Mimamsa and Vedanta. Charvaka, the founder of an atheistic materialist school, was prominent in North India between 400 B.C. and 1,000 A.D. Hinduism expanded at the expense of Buddhism.

Sanskritic culture went into decline after the end of this period. The early medieval Puranas helped establish a religious mainstream among the tribal societies undergoing enculturalization. The tenets of Brahmanic Hinduism underwent a radical transformation at the hands of various Vedic composers, resulting in the rise of a mainstream Hinduism that overshadowed all earlier traditions.

Though Islam came to India in the early 7th Century with the arrival of Arab traders and the conquest of northern India, it only started to become a major religion during the Muslim conquest of the Indian subcontinent. Because of the influx of Muslims, Buddhism declined and many Hindus converted to Islam. Muslim rulers destroyed Hindu temples and persecuted non-Muslims. During this time, Hinduism underwent other profound changes due to the influence of prominent teachers. Followers of the Bhakti movement, moved away from the abstract idea of an impersonal Brahman, towards the more accessible *avatars*, especially *Krishna* and *Rama*.

Indology, as an academic discipline studying Indian culture from a European perspective, became important in the 19th century. Academicians brought Vedic, Puranic and Tantric literature and philosophy to Europe and the United States. At the same time, groups such as the Theosophical Society, attempted to fuse Buddhist and Dharmaic philosophies, in order to institute societal reform. In the West, movements with Hindu origins swelled the ranks of religion. Swami Prabhupada, founder of ISKCON, translated Hinduism's foundational texts for modern audiences. This attracted followers in India and abroad. Others, such as Swami Yogananda and Rama have also been instrumental in raising the profiles of Yoga and Vedanta in the West. Today, modern movements, such as ISKCON attract large numbers of followers across the world.[20]

> *"Hinduism is a synthesis of the various religious ideas and influences from throughout India."*

Hinduism today is not the same as Hinduism five thousand years ago. The Hindu religion has evolved over the past five millennia of Indian religious history. It is a synthesis of the various religious ideas and influences from throughout India, representing hundreds of separate cultural, social, and tribal groups.

While different Hindu sects appear as independent religions, they regard themselves as divisions of the One Eternal Religion of India. Each considers itself the best and most favored channel of expression and interpretation.

THE HINDU CONCEPT OF GOD

Brahma is the highest form of divinity in Hindu religious thought. While Hindus venerate Brahma, Brahma is not a single entity or deity. Similar to Buddhism, Hinduism views Brahma as an intangible, ambiguous energy, called *prana*. Subservient to the idea of Brahma is the pantheon of millions of Hindu gods and goddesses. Although Hinduism caricaturizes Brahma as an impersonal, unknowable force, it incarnates itself in a Trinitarian triad of gods: Shiva, Vishnu and Krishna.

Shiva, or creator, is the Hindu fertility god who makes the crops grow. There is no mention of him in the Rig Veda. Nevertheless, around 300 BC, people began worshipping Shiva under another name for the Harappan god Rudra. Shiva (or Rudra) was less like a real man than Vishnu. People thought Shiva spent most of his time meditating (sitting and thinking) on top of Mount Kailas in the Himalayas. His mediation makes the spiritual energy that runs the universe.

---

[20]   Hinduism https://www.britannica.com/topic/Hinduism (Accessed October 14, 2022).

According to tradition, the Ganges River came out of the head of Shiva, and that made the river and its waters sacred. People went to swim in the Ganges if they were sick, so the holy water would make them better. Bulls are also sacred to Shiva, and because of this, most Hindus will not eat them.

Vishnu, or preserver, is another member of the Hindu triad of gods. He appears in the Rig Veda as a god. People began to worship Vishnu as an important god around 300 BC. Worship of Vishnu includes offering him flowers, incense, food, by praying to him or playing music. They did not usually sacrifice animals to Vishnu.

People thought of Vishnu as repeatedly reincarnating in different forms. Sometimes Vishnu appears in the form of Krishna, which was one of his reincarnations. Another reincarnation of Vishnu is the god Rama. Rama's story appears in the great poem, the *Ramayana*, written about 300 BC.

Krishna or destroyer is the final member of the triad of the Hindu gods. He was just one of the many forms of the god Vishnu. Krishna is sometimes a reincarnation of Vishnu. He appears in many complicated stories. Sometimes he is pictured as a child, while at other times he appears as a flute-player who calls people's souls. There are stories in which he involves himself in love affairs with Hindu goddesses, and at other times, he is portrayed as a great leader. One important appearance of Krishna is in the Bhagavad Gita, where he is the god who tells the young prince how to act, and what is good and what is bad.[21] Contemporary Hinduism continues to be polytheistic, worshipping many gods. Nevertheless, this triad of deities continues to be the prominent members of the pantheon.

THE BELIEFS OF HINDUISM

Polytheism It is important to our study to remember that Hinduism is a *polytheistic* belief system. *Polytheism is the belief in many gods.* The word "poly" comes from the Greek word for "many". "Theos" is the Greek word for "god." Polytheism has perhaps been the dominant theistic view in human history. The best-known example of polytheism in ancient times is Greek and Roman mythology (Zeus, Apollo, Aphrodite, and Poseidon).

---

[21] Hindu Deities https://www.khanacademy.org/humanities/art-asia/beginners-guide-asian-culture/hindu-art- culture/a/hindu-deities (Accessed October 14, 2022)

The clearest modern example of polytheism is Hinduism, which has over 330 million gods and goddesses. Although Hinduism is polytheistic in practice, it is also pantheistic in its belief in the impersonal life energy source called Brahma.

Teaching The main texts of Hinduism are the Vedas (considered most important), Upanishads, the Mahabharata, and the Ramayana. These writings contain hymns, incantations, philosophies, rituals, poems, and stories from which Hindus base their beliefs. Other texts used in Hinduism include the Brahmanas, the Sutras, and the Aranyakas.

"Hinduism has over 330 million gods and goddesses."

Hinduism is a conglomeration of various religious schools of thought. Some of these influences can make Hinduism seem confusing. For instance, although Hinduism is a polytheistic belief system, some also consider it to be:

1. Monistic -- Only one god exists; Sankara's school

2. Pantheistic -- Only one divine god exists; God is identical with the world; Brahmanism

3. Panentheistic -- The world is part of god; Ramanuja's School

4. Theistic -- Only one divine god exists; Bhakti School.

With such diversity of thought, one may wonder what makes Hinduism, "Hindu" in the first place. About the only real issue is whether a particular school recognizes the Vedas as sacred. If it does, then it is Hindu. If not, then it is not Hindu.

The *Vedas* are more than theology books. They contain a rich and colorful "theo-mythology." This religious mythology deliberately interweaves myth, theology, and history to achieve a story-form religious root. "Theo-mythology" is so deeply rooted in India's history and culture that to reject the Vedas is to reject India. Therefore, Hinduism rejects a belief system if it does not embrace Indian culture to some extent. If a system accepts Indian culture and its theo-mythical history, then it is "Hindu" even if its theology is theistic, nihilistic, or atheistic.

This openness to contradiction can be a headache for Westerners who seek logical consistency and rational defensibility in their religious views. However, to be fair, Christians are no more logical when they claim to believe in Yahweh yet live life as practical atheists, denying Christ. For the Hindu, the conflict is genuine logical contradiction. For the Christian, the conflict is more likely simple hypocrisy.

View of Man. Because Brahma is universal, *Hinduism asserts that all humanity is divine. Atman,* or self, is one with Brahman. All of reality outside Brahman is mere illusion. The spiritual goal of a Hindu is to become one with Brahma, thus ceasing to exist in the form of "individual self." "Moksha," is freedom from self. Until moksha takes place, a Hindu believes that they will repeatedly reincarnate so they may work towards self-realization of the truth that only Brahman exists and nothing else. Reincarnation occurs through *karma.* Karma is a principle of cause and effect governed by nature's balance. What one did in the past affects what happens in the future.[22]

Existence of Spirits Also intrinsic to Hinduism's structure is *the existence of lower deities or spirits.* The Hindu scriptures refer to celestial entities called *Devas* or *Devi* in feminine form. *Devatā,* in Hindi, means "the shining ones." The English translation of this phrase means "gods" or "heavenly beings". *Devas* are an integral part of Hindu culture and appear in art, architecture and icons. Mythological stories about them appear in the Vedic scriptures as well. These spirits course through the air, sometimes in flying chariots and will at times incarnate themselves as *avatars* (devas who possess humans), to restore dharma (right teaching), and guide humans to *moshka* or nirvana.

View of God Although Hinduism is polytheistic in nature, it has varying ideas of Brahma, or "god". Its view of God is complex and is part of each tradition and philosophy. Most Hindus believe the soul of every person, called the *atman,* is eternal. According to the monistic and pantheistic theologies of Hinduism, such as the Advaita Vedanta School, the *atman* is indistinct from Brahman, the supreme spirit. Therefore, this school is non-dualist. The goal of life, according to the Advaita School, is

---

22   What is Hinduism and what do Hindus believe? http://www.gotquestions.org/ hinduism.html (accessed November 8, 2022)

to realize that one's *atman* is identical with Brahman, the supreme soul. The Upanishads state that whoever becomes fully aware of the *atman* as the innermost core of one's own self identifies with Brahman and reaches *moksha* (liberation or freedom).

Dualistic schools such as Dvaita and Bhakti, understand Brahma as a Supreme Being who possesses personality, and they worship him as Vishnu, Brahma, or Shiva, depending on the sect. The *atman* is dependent on God, while *moksha* depends on love towards God and on God's grace. When God appears as the supreme personal being, rather than as the infinite principle, he manifests himself as *Ishvara*, "The Lord", "The Auspicious One" or "The Supreme Lord".

Belief in Reincarnation Fundamental to Hindu belief is the concept of reincarnation. To the Hindu, reincarnation is a complex principle linking with the three ideas of *karma, samsara and moksha*. *Karma* translates as action, work, or deed, and is an effect of "moral law and cause and effect". According to the Upanishads, an individual develops *sanskaras* (impressions) from actions, whether physical or mental. The *linga sharira*, a body more subtle than the physical one, retains impressions, carrying them over into the next life, establishing a unique trajectory for the individual. Thus, karma is a universal and neutral idea that is an intrinsic ingredient of the philosophy of reincarnation. It defines one's personality, characteristics, and family as well. Karma binds together the notions of free will and destiny.

This cycle of action, reaction, birth, death and rebirth is a continuum called *samsara*. The notion of reincarnation and karma is a strong premise in Hindu thought. The Bhagavad Gita states, *"As a person puts on new clothes and discards old and torn clothes, an embodied soul enters new material bodies, leaving the old ones"*. (B. G. 2:22)

Samsara provides ephemeral pleasures, which lead people to desire rebirth to enjoy the pleasures of a perishable body. However, escaping *samsara* through *moksha* is the only way to ensure lasting happiness and peace. Many think that after several reincarnations, an *atman* eventually seeks unity with the cosmic spirit (Brahman).

"Yoga is the embodiment of Hindu belief and worship".

Eternity There are different views regarding *moksha*, or *nirvana*, in Hinduism. Most Hindus believe that the ultimate goal of life is nirvana. Some see it as realization of union with god, or as eternal relationship with god. Others see life's goal as realization of the unity of all existence, perfect unselfishness and knowledge of the Self. The goal of life is to attain perfect mental peace and detachment from worldly desires. Such realization liberates one from *samsara* and ends the cycle of rebirth.[23]

Yoga, the highest form of Worship Yoga is the embodiment of Hindu belief and worship. The two intractably intertwine. In whatever way a Hindu defines the goal of life, sages have taught several yogas for reaching that goal. Texts dedicated to Yoga include the *Bhagavad Gita*, the *Yoga Sutras*, and the *Hatha Yoga Pradipika*. Their philosophical and historic basis appears in the Upanishads. Paths that one can follow to achieve the spiritual goal of life (*moksha* or *nirvana*) include:

- Bhakti Yoga (the path of love and devotion)
- Karma Yoga (the path of right action)
- Raja Yoga (the path of meditation)
- Jnana Yoga (the path of wisdom)

An individual may prefer one or some yogas to others, according to his or her inclination and understanding. Some devotional schools teach that *bhakti* is the only practical path to achieve spiritual perfection. Other Hindus, believe that the world is currently in the *Kali Yoga* (one of four epochs that are part of the Yoga cycle. Interestingly, one practice of yoga does not exclude the practice of others. Many schools believe the different yogas naturally blend into and aid other forms of yoga. For example, the practice of *jnana yoga*, is thought to lead to pure love (the goal of *bhakti yoga*), and vice versa. Someone practicing deep meditation (such as in *raja yoga*) must embody the core principles of *karma yoga*, *jnana yoga* and *bhakti yoga*, whether directly or indirectly.

World religion expert Professor Ninan Smart notes the problems innate to present-day Hindu systems: "Someone might ask, "What is the essence of Hinduism? This is a difficult question to answer. There are orthodox Hindus who deny the existence of God. While there are those who do not

---

[23] Oneness and Pluralism: Hinduism's Essence https://www.hinduamerican.org/hinduism-basics (Accessed October 14, 2022)

deny the existence of god, they relegate him to a second place. They see God as an illusory form of the Absolute. Amid this variety of theological views, what remains necessary to Hindu belief? Central to Hinduism are the doctrines of rebirth and that of an eternal soul. It pictures the world as a place where the immortal spirit endlessly travels through the circle of reincarnation. This idea has dominated the Indian imagination for three millennia. Added to this, is a complex social system that has given shape to the religion of the subcontinent over a long period. [24]

SUMMARY AND CONCLUSIONS

To summarize the major tenets of Hinduism, we must understand its essentials. First, Hinduism is polytheistic and worships a pantheon of millions of gods and goddesses. These gods unite in a higher expression of religious essence called Brahma. Brahma consists of a universal force made up of a mysterious all pervasive energy called *prana*. In most sects of Hinduism, Brahma incarnates itself in a triad of gods consisting of Shiva, Vishnu and Krishna. The essential doctrine of Hinduism is *reincarnation* and is an integral idea related to *karma*. Karma is a belief that the next reincarnate state is dependent on the individual's goodness in the present life. Hinduism incorporates a belief in spirits, called *devas*, and exalted humans called *avatars*. These spirits interact with humans and can possess the worshiper's body to manifest themselves. The most visible expression of Hindu worship is the practice of *Yoga*. Yoga is a mind-body exercise that promotes the connection between the spirit world and the worshipper. Hinduism is *syncretistic* and is a synthesis of hundreds of religions that merged across India.

"The essential doctrine of Hinduism is reincarnation".

Hinduism shares many ties with touch therapies. Both believe in a Universal Life Energy that is an impersonal expression of all living matter. The therapist directs this energy, or *prana,* to the patient to produce healing. This concept is borrowed directly from Hinduism. Both Hinduism and

---

[24]   Martin, Walter. *Kingdom of the Cults*, Bethany House, Minneapolis, Minnesota, 1997. pp. 390, 391.

touch therapies believe in contacting incorporeal spirits for guidance. Many alternative therapies use yoga as a means for connecting with the pranaic universe. By clearing the mind though meditation, and the ascetic manipulation of the body, they open their spirits to channel Hindu gods and goddesses. Just as Hinduism incorporates numerous religions, alternative therapies also incorporate whatever religious views suits its needs.

Hinduism, with its broad diversity and inclusivity, is not compatible with Christianity. It replaces the biblical doctrine of the Trinity with a triad of Hindu gods. It replaces a personal relationship with God the Father with an impersonal and ambiguous Bramhic figure. Through the teaching of reincarnation and karma, it denies the work of Christ on Calvary, the need for repentance and faith, as well as the need of a Savior. Hinduism replaces resurrection with reincarnation, and both grace and faith with human works. Hindus will never experience peace with God despite their continual practice of yoga. C. S. Lewis wisely observed that at the end of all religious quests one must choose between Hinduism and Christianity. The former absorbs all others and the latter excludes them. Peace with God cannot happen by looking inside oneself but by looking up to Him of whom Moses and the prophets did write — Jesus of Nazareth, the Christ and Son of God.

STUDY QUESTIONS

HINDUISM'S SEARCH FOR THE ONE TRUE GOD

1. How did our present-day health system develop?

2. What I Hinduism and how did it develop?

3. What is Polytheism?

4. What is the Hindu concept of God?

5. What is Hinduism's concept of humans?

6. What are devas and what is their purpose?

7. How does the Hindu belief in Brahma differ from Buddhism's concept of Nirvana?

8. What is the role of karma and reincarnation in Hinduism? How are they different than in Buddhism?

9. What is the purpose of Yoga in Hinduism?

10. What similarities are there between Hinduism and Touch Therapies?

11. How does Hinduism differ from Christianity?

CHAPTER 4
THE PERPLEXING IDEAS OF THEOSOPHY

CHAPTER 4
THE PERPLEXING IDEAS OF THEOSOPHY

*"All religions, arts and sciences are branches
of the same tree".*
— Albert Einstein

We have seen in the past two chapters that touch therapies are not a medical modalities they are in essence, religious belief systems. Steeped in Buddhism and Hinduism, touch therapies share philosophies with Eastern religions that have no connection to medical paradigms that derive from Christian values.

Touch medicine is syncretistic and not only incorporates beliefs from Eastern thought, but as we will soon find out, builds on occult practices as well. One occult system that is foundational to touch therapies is Theosophy. Since Theosophy plays such a vital role in integrative medicine, we will examine its key figures, its historical development, and its teachings to understand the link between it and touch therapies.

HISTORY AND DEVELOPMENT OF THEOSOPHY

Theosophy is a doctrine of religious philosophy and metaphysics originating with Helena Petrovna Blavatsky (1831–91). Theosophy holds that all religions are attempts by the "Spiritual Hierarchy" to help humanity evolve and reach perfection. It teaches that each religion has a portion of the truth.

Organized in New York City in 1875, the Society's principal founder was Helena Petrovna Blavatsky. Helena was the first Russian woman naturalized as an American citizen. The other predominate figure was Henry Steel

Olcott, a prominent lawyer and journalist who became the first President of the Society. Madame Blavatsky was a Russian of noble birth, whose mother was a social novelist and whose grandmother was an amateur scientist. As a young woman, she traveled all over the world in search of wisdom about the nature of life and human existence. Eventually, Blavatsky brought the ancient spiritual wisdom of the East to the modern West, where it was virtually unknown. Her writings became the first expositions of modern Theosophy.

Colonel Olcott was a veteran of the Civil War. He had been a special investigator into corruption in the armed services. Following the war, he was a member of the commission appointed to investigate the assassination of President Abraham Lincoln. Olcott was also an internationally renowned agricultural authority. He was especially adept at weaving the timeless wisdom of the cultures of both East and West, applying it to everyday life, and built the Theosophical Society into an international organization.

"Theosophy teaches that each religion has a portion of the truth".

Associated with Blavatsky and Olcott, was, a young New York attorney William Quan Judge. Other important figures gained interest in the philosophy espoused by Madame Blavatsky as well. The latter included General Abner Doubleday, the legendary founder of baseball, and the famous inventor Thomas Alva Edison.

Because of its ties to Hinduism, Madame Blavatsky and Colonel Olcott moved to India in 1879, where the Society spread rapidly. In 1882, they established the Society's international headquarters in Adyar, a suburb of Madras (currently Chennai), where it has remained since. The couple also visited Sri Lanka, where Olcott was so active in promoting social welfare among oppressed Buddhists that even now he is a national hero of that land. Today, the Society has members in almost 70 countries around the world.

The U. S. administrative center of the sect called "Olcott", in honor of the President-Founder, is located in Wheaton, Illinois. Approximately 110 study centers in major cities of the country carry on active Theosophical work. A considerable number of members belong to the national center.[25]

---

[25] Brief History of the Theosophical Society https://www.theosophical.org/ts-network/79-about-us-sp-709/society/1040-history-of-the-theosophical-society (Accessed Nov. 8, 2022).

MADAM HELENA BLAVATSKY

Theosophy claims to be a universal religion with a distinctive nature. However, any careful study of its eclectic background reveals that much of its "original theology" is from sources in Hinduism, Christianity and Buddhism. The American history of Theosophy began with a young mystic named Madam Helena Blavatsky, in New York City.

At the age of seventeen, Helena married the czarist general Blavatsky. Blavatsky was a cultured man many years her senior, whom she promptly left after only three months of marriage. It is a known fact that Helena Blavatsky was notoriously short of patience and had a violent temper. One of her biographers records that she married General Blavatsky merely to spite her acid-tongued governess. In a moment of sarcasm, her governess declared that even the noble old man would not marry a shrew like Helena. To her credit, Madam Blavatsky repented hastily of her revenge on the governess, but she had already beguiled the general into matrimony.

Shortly after her separation from General Blavatsky, Helena embarked on a long career of travel that eventually led her into the field of mystical religion. She studied from Tibet, India, and Egypt, as well as Texas, Louisiana, Cuba, and Canada, settling eventually in New York. While she was there, Blavatsky founded The Theosophical Society in 1875.

In 1879, Madam Blavatsky left the United States for India, and later died in London, England, in 1891. W. Q. Judge split the Society in 1895, and divided it into the "Universal Brotherhood and Theosophical Society" and "The Theosophical Society in America." Madam Blavatsky held Judge in the highest esteem. Judge wore her mantle of leadership as president of the Aryan Theosophical Society until 1896, when he died.

Among other accomplishments, Madam Blavatsky also founded the Esoteric School of Theosophy in London in 1888. During her travels in India and England, she profoundly influenced Annie Wood Besant. Besant eventually took over leadership of the school after the deaths of Blavatsky, Judge, and his successor, Catherine Tingley.

Helena Blavatsky was a woman of tremendous physical proportions with piercing, almost hypnotic eyes. She ruled the Theosophists during her lifetime and even after her death, through her literary works. She accomplished this through her book, *"The Secret Doctrine"*, which Theosophists still consider as divinely inspired oracles and instructions.

Blavatsky's first major book *Isis Unveiled* (1877) presented ideas mainly from the Eastern wisdom tradition based on her extensive travels in Asia, Europe and the Middle East. Her second major work *The Secret Doctrine* (1888), contains a commentary on *The Book of Dzyan*. She called this, an *Unwritten Secret Doctrine* or *Wisdom Religion Allotted to Man*. This book describes the underlying basis of all the religions of humanity. These writings, along with the *Key to Theosophy* and *The Voice of the Silence* are essential texts for genuine students.

ANNIE BESANT

Annie Besant (1847-1933) was the most prominent of all British Theosophical luminaries. She intended to become a bright star in the political fortunes of India. Among her many accomplishments, Besant founded the Central Hindu College at Benares, India, in 1898. She founded the Indian Home Rule League in 1916. In the year 1917, she became president of the Indian National Congress and was held in high regard as a powerful figure in Indian politics.

In 1889, Mrs. Besant, a native of London, became enthralled by the personality and teachings of Madam Blavatsky and became a devout pupil and disciple. Annie Besant firmly believed the teachings of Madam Blavatsky represented the true doctrines of the cult and always lauded the writings of the Russian seer.

Mrs. Besant had several idiosyncrasies, and took a mystical approach to both life and religion. In 1925, she claimed that her adopted son Krishnamurti, was an Indian mystic, and gave him the title of "Messianic Leader and Reincarnation of the World Teacher."

The new Messiah, however, renounced this grandeur on November 20, 1931 at Krotana, California, headquarters of the American branch of Theosophy. Annie Besant died in 1933, at which time George Arundale and C. Jinara Jodosa succeeded to the presidency of the American Society.[26]

---

[26]   Martin, Walter. *Kingdom of the Cults*, Bethany House, Minneapolis, Minnesota, 2003, pp.284, 285.

CHARLES WEBSTER LEADBEATER

Charles Leadbeater was born in Stockport, Cheshire, in 1854. Public records show that he was an only child. By 1861, the family had moved to London. His father, Charles Sr., died of tuberculosis in 1862, when Charles was only eight years old. Four years later, another misfortune struck the family when a bank in which they had their savings collapsed. Without finances for college, Charles had to look for work after graduating high school to support him and his mother. He held various clerical jobs over time. During the evenings, he educated himself. For example, he studied astronomy and had a 12-inch reflector telescope to observe the heavens at night. He also taught himself French, Latin and Greek.

His uncle was a prominent Anglican cleric. Under his uncle's influence, Charles was ordained as an Anglican priest in 1879 at Farnham, England. He lived with his mother at Bramshott in a cottage that his uncle had built, where he became Curate. Charles was a minister, teacher and youth leader who many remember as "a bright, cheerful, and kindhearted man." After reading about the séances of medium Daniel Dunglas Home (1833-1886), Leadbeater developed an active interest in spiritualism. After the death of his mother, he invested himself in this interest, devoting himself to contacting his deceased mother.

Joining the Theosophical Society in London, Leadbeater continued his occult investigations and in May 1894, did his first Past Life reading. He became one of the most well known speakers in the Theosophical Society and was Secretary of the London Lodge. In 1895, he and Annie Besant began "occult investigations into the cosmos. He relates that they "frequently visited the Ascended Masters together in their astral bodies."

After Leadbeater's return to England in 1906, he took the fourteen-year-old son of the Corresponding Secretary of the Esoteric Section in Chicago, with him to San Francisco on his first lecture tour. The teenage boy confessed to his parents the reason why he was angry with his mentor was that Leadbeater encouraged him to masturbate with him. Almost simultaneously, a son of another Theosophical official in Chicago charged Leadbeater with the same offense. There appeared to be no collusion between the two boys. Excommunicated from the Society for two years, the International Sections voted for Leadbeater's readmission in 1908 and he accepted.

"There is a population of human-like beings on the planet Mars".

Leadbeater's most well known accomplishment was the discovery of the prophet Krishnamurti. This discovery took place on the private beach that formed part of the Theosophical headquarters in Adyar, India in 1909. Krishnamurti and his family had been living in the headquarters for a few months before his discovery. He was to be the vessel for the indwelling of the coming "World Teacher" that many Theosophists were expecting. This new teacher, in the pattern of Moses, Buddha, Zarathustra (Zoroaster), Christ, and Muhammad would introduce a new dispensation.

Leadbeater remains influential today in his work with clairvoyance and Hinduism through his books, *The Chakras* and *Man,* and *Visible and Invisible.* These deal with the human aura and chakras, and writings on the Sacraments of the Liberal Catholic Church. Leadbeater's clairvoyance was not without grave error. In his book *The Inner Life,* he writes "there is a population of human-like beings on the planet Mars".[27]

ALICE BAILEY

Alice Bailey was born to a wealthy aristocratic British family, and as a member of the Anglican Church, received a thorough Christian education. She described a lonely and "over-sheltered" childhood and was unhappy despite the luxury of her physical circumstances.

In her autobiography, she relates that as a child she was unhappy and did not find life worth living. Because of this, she attempted suicide three times: the first at the age of five, the second at age 11, and the third at an unspecified time before age 15. She wrote that after her third attempt, she lost interest in the idea, but that she "always understood the impulse."

On June 30, 1895, at the age of 15, a stranger visited Bailey. She describes him as "a tall man, dressed in European clothes and wearing a turban." He told her she needed to develop self-control to prepare for certain work planned for her to do. She supposed this individual was Jesus, but later identified him as *Master Koot Hoomi.*

At age 22, Bailey did evangelistic work with the YMCA and the British Army. This took her to India where, in 1907, she met her future husband,

---

[27] Leadbeater, Charles Webster https://adb.anu.edu.au/biography/leadbeater-charles-webster-7132 (Accessed October 14, 2022).

Walter Evans. Together, they moved to America where Evans became an Episcopalian priest. However, their marriage did not last. She stated that her husband mistreated her and in one of his fits of temper, threw her down the stairs. Bailey sued for and received a divorce. She left with their three children after formal separation in 1915. Bailey experienced a difficult period in which she worked as a factory hand to support herself and the children.

Bailey's break was not only with her Episcopalian husband, but also with Christianity. In her autobiography, she wrote, "a rabid, orthodox Christian worker had become a well-known occult teacher."

In 1915, Bailey discovered the Theosophical Society and the work of Helena Petrovna Blavatsky. The Theosophical Society states that Bailey became involved in 1917. Theosophist Joy Mills records that in 1918 Bailey became a member of the Esoteric Section of the society. Theosophist Bruce F. Campbell notes, "She quickly rose to a position of influence in the society, moving to its headquarters at Krotona in Hollywood. Later, Bailey became editor of its magazine, *The Messenger*, and member of the committee responsible for Krotona."

Alice Bailey claimed to recognize Koot Hoomi, the master who had visited her in her childhood, from a portrait she saw in the Shrine Room of the Theosophical Society. She wrote much about those she called the "Masters of Wisdom." She believed them to be a society of enlightened sages guided by "the Christ." She felt that her writings were an effort to clarify the nature of these Masters, and their work.

With her second husband, Foster Bailey, Alice formed the Arcane School that later became the Lucis Trust. She accepted the basic Theosophical views on karma, reincarnation, ascended masters, a divine plan, and humanity's divine status. Known mostly for her writings, she hammered home the central idea the East is the true home of spiritual knowledge and occult wisdom. Bailey continued her work up to her death in 1948. Her husband Foster remained head of the head of the Lucis Trust until his death in 1977.[28]

BARBARA BRENNAN

Barbara Ann Brennan, born February 19, 1939 is an American author, spiritual healer and businessperson. She works in the controversial field of "energy healing". Brennan coined the term Higher Sense Perception to describe her work.

[28] Bailey, Alice A. *The Unfinished Autobiography*. Lucis Trust. 1951. pp 267

Brennan originally trained as a physicist. She received her Bachelor of Science degree in Physics in 1962 from the University of Wisconsin-Madison. Two years later, she received her Master's in Atmospheric Physics from the same institution. Following her education, she worked as a research scientist at NASA's Goddard Space Flight Center.

Her first book, *Hands of Light: a Guide to Healing through the Human Energy Field*, became popular in 1989. It is a "classic" in spiritual healing. There are reputedly over one million copies of her book in print in 22 languages. Brennan's books illustrate drawings of auras and energy fields, and her descriptions of how human energy fields interact with one another. Her ideas on healing draw on the views of Theosophists such as C. W. Leadbeater and Alice Bailey. Brennan popularized a seven-layer model of the energy field, each layer constructed of different frequencies. Brennan views the chakras (energy vortices) as transformers of cosmic energy that enable healthy functioning of the individual's psychophysical make-up. Her unique contribution is the identification of two rows of chakras. She claims that these pairs exist in the anterior and posterior portions of the body. The front chakras relate to Feeling, the rear chakras with Will, and the upper three with Intellect.

> *"Her books draw on messages channeled from Heyoan, who she claims to believe to be her spirit guide".*

Brennan claims to receive intuitive messages about her clients during sessions. She also claims to see repetitive patterns in the energy consciousness of her clients. These ideas are indicative of the difficulties underlying her books. Her books draw on messages channeled from *Heyoan*, who she claims to believe to be her *spirit guide*.

In 1982, she established the Barbara Brennan School of Healing, designed to train professional healers. The school is located in Florida, and licensed by the State of Florida Commission for Independent Education. It offers a Bachelor of Science degree and a Professional Studies diploma in "Brennan Healing Science".[29]

---

29   Barbara Brennan https://en-academic.com/dic.nsf/enwiki/11257323 (Accessed October 14, 2022).

BELIEFS AND TEACHING OF THEOSOPHY

Although the biographical information included here is extensive, it is an anecdotal means to explain Theosophy's origins, development and its beliefs. Since Theosophy is so significant to the spiritual groundwork of touch therapies, it is imperative that we understand it.

The Theosophical Society of America is not a large organization and only has about 3,900 members with just over 100 "Lodges". However, its influence in the area of touch therapies is staggering. Theosophy has *Three Declared Objects* as goals. These are:

- To form a nucleus of the universal brotherhood of humanity, without distinction of race, creed, sex, caste, or color.
- To encourage the comparative study of religion, philosophy, and science.
- To investigate unexplained laws of nature and the powers latent in humanity.

What source do Theosophists base their beliefs on? Beside the writings of its founders, Theosophy states there are no other sacred books. Revelation comes from *"adepts"*, or *spirit beings*. These spirits are "spiritually perfect, intellectually, and physically, the flower of human and all evolution.'" Mrs. Blavatsky was the first individual in Theosophy who received messages from the *adepts* and passed them on to the world.

Theosophy's current beliefs and teachings are a synthesis of the writings of its founders and a mixture of Hindu, Buddhist, Spiritualist and Christian beliefs. Doctrinally, it most closely resembles Hinduism. The influence of Hindu thought is a key component of its teaching:

- One Life pervades and sustains the universe.
- The universe is the manifestation of an eternal, boundless and immutable Reality beyond the range of human understanding.
- The entire system of the universe, visible and invisible, is the scene of the great scheme of evolution. In evolution, life moves to ever more expressive, more responsive awareness, and a more unified consciousness.

- The human consciousness (also called spirit or soul) is in essence identical with the one supreme Reality, which Ralph Waldo Emerson called the "Over soul." This includes each person and unites us with one another.

- The gradual unfolding of this latent divine Reality within us takes place by the process of reincarnation, which is an aspect of the cyclic law. it is demonstrated everywhere in nature, by periods of activity alternating with periods of rest and assimilation. As Saint Paul says, whatever we sow, we will inevitably reap. This is the law of karma, by which we weave our own destiny through the ages. It is the great hope for humanity, for it gives us the opportunity to create our future by what we do in the present.

- The human pilgrimage takes us from our source in the One through experience of the many, back to union with the One Divine Reality. This realization is enlightenment.[30]

CONTROVERSY WITH CHRISTIANITY

Theosophists attempt to "baptize" their beliefs in colloquial Christian semantics because they recognize the Christian milieu in which they exist and operate. The truth is that Theosophy openly opposes Christianity in most of its writings.

About God Regarding the existence of God, they write, "We reject the idea of a personal God" (H. P. Blavatsky, *Key to Theosophy*, Point Loma, California, Aryan Theosophical Press, 1913). "We believe in a universal divine principle, the root of all, from which all proceeds, and within which all will be absorbed at the end of the great cycle of being"

On Humanity Theosophy radically reinterprets the Scriptural view of humanity, the means of Salvation and our eternal destiny. Krishnamurti said that, Theosophists teach that man consists of seven parts: 1. The body; 2. Vitality; 3. Astral body; 4. Animal soul; 5. Human soul; 6. Spiritual soul; and 7. Spirit. "Man is God, for you are God, and you will only what God wills. You must dig deep down into yourself to find the God within you. Then listen to His voice which is your voice" (Krishnamurti, *At the Feet of the Master*, p. 10).

---

[30] The Voice of the Silence https://www.theosociety.org/pasadena/voice/voice.htm (Accessed October 14, 2022)

> *"Theosophists attempt to "baptize" their beliefs in colloquial Christian terms."*

About Salvation Man is evolving individually and corporately. Salvation occurs when man's seventh stage takes place, involving progressing from one body to another based on his own self-effort. This is the law of Karma.

Jesus Christ Concerning the Person of Jesus Christ Madam Blavatsky wrote, "For Christ, the true esoteric savior, is no man but the DIVINE PRINCIPLE in every human being" (H. P. Blavatsky, *Studies in Occultism*, Theosophical University Press, n.d., p. 134).

Eternal Life Instead of every Christian's hope in the resurrection of the body, Theosophy replaces it with the hopeless cycle of reincarnation. "No one is to blame except us for our birth conditions, our character, our opportunities, and our abilities. All of these are because of the working out of forces we have set going either in this life or in former lives".

God's Word Finally, Theosophy plainly states that it rejects God's Word, the Bible. "I confine myself to the Hindu Scriptures. I state these scriptures and the Hindu religion is the origin of all scriptures and all religions." (Annie Besant, *The Daily Chronicle*, April 9, 1894).

When we examine Theosophical beliefs, we discover it is contrary to Christianity. It may try to borrow theological jargon to appeal to Western beliefs, but under scrutiny, it fails to embrace a single concept of Christian spirituality. There is, no possibility of reconciliation between the two, since the followers of Theosophy extol Buddhist and Brahmanic theories while Christians follow Jesus Christ alone.[31]

Regarding Heaven and Hell According to the literature of the theosophical cult written by Blavatsky, Besant, and Leadbeater, there is a great fraternity of *"Mahatmas"* or *"Masters."* They are reincarnations whose dwelling place is somewhere in the far reaches of remote Tibet. These writers claim that divine beings possessed Madam Blavatsky and utilized her to reach the world with the truths of the great religions. In this imaginative picture of the afterlife, Theosophists describe seven planes of progression that the souls of individuals must pass through on their way

---

[31] Handbook of Today's Religions - Clover Sites https://pdf4pro.com/view/handbook-of-today-s-religions-clover-sites-303ace.html (Accessed October 15, 2022).

to "heaven" or *Devachan*. In the final analysis, the Theosophist view of heaven is in reality the *nirvana* of Buddhism where the personality absorbs and eventually extinguishes individual cognizance.

Theosophists also have their "hell," which, oddly enough, resembles the Roman Catholic idea of purgatory. They picture indescribable tortures and degrees of degradation. The name for this intermediate state of existence, where the departed soul suffers for their past sins, is *Kamaloka*. Kamaloka is an anteroom where souls linger while awaiting reincarnation. Theosophical writings describe it as "gloomy, heavy, dreary, and depressing to an inconceivable extent".

About the Soul Theosophy's esoteric cosmology claims the universe orders itself according to the number seven. This principle applies to the doctrine of reincarnation. The reincarnation of the consciousness of the *monad* or spirit, coalesces in seven etheric bodies. The first body is *Sthula-sarira* and refers to the physical body. The second body is the *Linga-Sarira*, and refers to the astral body. The third body is *prana*. Prana is the "breath of life" and refers to the energy that comprises the soul. The fourth principle is *Kama*, that is the seat of the living impulses, desires, and aspirations. The fifth body is *manas,* or the reincarnating ego, immortal in essence. The sixth principle body is *Buddhi.* The qualities of the buddhic principle when awakened are higher judgment, instant understanding, discrimination, intuition, love that has no bounds, and consequent universal forgiveness. The seventh is *Atman*. Atman is the knowledge of "I am" or pure cognition, the abstract idea of self.[32]

SUMMARY AND CONCLUSIONS

Headquartered in Wheaton Illinois, the Theosophy Society of America is a movement that began almost 135 years ago. Its beliefs and practices embrace Hinduism although it has strong connections to Buddhism and Spiritism. Theosophists attempt to make their beliefs palatable to the Christian mind, yet deny Christian teaching at every turn. Sadly, several of its founders were at one time involved in Christian ministry and service. One was a British cleric turned spiritualist and pedophile. Another was an evangelist who became an ardent advocate of Spiritism. All of them fell away from their faith in Christ and delved into false religion and the occult.

---

[32] The Theosophical Society in Australia: Some Key Ideas https://theosophicalsociety.org.au/statics/key-ideas (Accessed October 14, 2022).

Theosophy embraces Hindu beliefs in good works through karma, a cyclical view of life through death, rebirth and unrelenting reincarnation. Its goal is nirvana or union with the universal force of the galaxy that combines all energy.

Theosophy practices Spiritism. It promotes the belief in the existence of *adepts* or spirits and communication with them by utilizing clairvoyance, clairaudience and mediumship. It also uses automatic writing, Past Life interpretation, reading of *auras*, astral projection and occult methods of healing.

"Theosophy adopts any religious system or belief that furthers its goals".

Although Theosophy steeps itself in Eastern religion and esoteric practice, it tries to appeal to nominal Christians by borrowing its language. Theosophy by its own admission is anything but Christian. One other interesting aspect of Theosophy is that its leaders adopt any religious system or belief that furthers its goals. At heart, it is a chameleon. In a single breath, its writers quote from Scripture, Hinduism's *Bagahvita* and Buddhism's *sutras* to embellish their lies. Theosophists identify themselves by their use of inclusive language and adaptability of their faith!

It is interesting to observe the broad influence of Theosophy on touch therapies. Several architects of touch therapies were leaders within the Theosophical Society of America. One such architect, Dora Kunz, was both president of the Theosophical Society, and editor-in-chief of its publishing house. Kunz is also co-founder of the integrative therapy of Therapeutic Touch. Is it any wonder that Theosophical ideas and aberrations significantly influence touch therapies?

Popular Theosophist personality, Barbara Brennan has probably done as much as any other individual to promote the use of occult methods of healing in health care. Through her writings, lectures and educational facilities in Florida, she is penetrating the area of medicine. Her classes focus on spiritual methods of healing that incorporate spirit guides, reading of auras, and implementation of the Eastern models of the *chakra system* and *energy medicine*. She touch therapies borrows liberally from the teachings of Theosophy. Because of her credentialing and focus on education, Brennan has been successful in introducing spiritual ideas of healing into the medical field. This is why we see that touch therapies are not medicine at all, but are a belief system diametrically opposed to faith in Christ.

STUDY QUESTIONS

THE PERPLEXING IDEAS OF THEOSOPHY

1. Discuss the life and contribution of Madam Helena Blavatsky to Theosophy.

2. Who is Annie Besant and what part did she play in the formation of Theosophy?

3. Who is Charles Leadbeater and what is his impact on Theosophy?

4. Who is Alice Bailey and what is her role in Theosophy?

5. How did Barbara Brennan attempt to legitimatize her Theosophical teachings?

6. What are the major teachings of theosophy?

7. How do Theosophy's teachings differ from Christianity?

8. What three religions form the basis of Theosophy? Share some of their influences.

9. Why is Theosophy so important in the development of Touch Therapies?

CHAPTER 5

THE EVILS OF SPIRITISM

CHAPTER 5
THE EVILS OF SPIRITISM

"There are two equal and opposite errors into which our race can fall about the devils. One is to disbelieve in their existence. The other is to believe, and to feel an excessive and unhealthy interest in them. They themselves are equally pleased by both errors and hail a materialist or a magician with the same delight.
— C. S. Lewis

We have seen that touch therapies are a hodgepodge of Eastern religious ideas and Theosophy. The next step necessary to understanding touch therapies and alternative medicine is to see that they also contain ingredients of the occult. As we will see, touch therapies link to the dark art of Spiritism. As believers in Christ Jesus, we understand that healing is the prerogative of the Holy Spirit. Whenever we look to other sources to experience physical healing, we are in essence looking outside the sphere of God's provision for our wholeness. In the end, we find ourselves turning instead to the power of the occult.

PRECURSORS TO SPIRITISM

Emanuel Swedenborg (January 29, 1688 – March 29, 1772) was a Swedish scientist, philosopher, seer, and theologian. Swedenborg had a prolific career as an inventor and scientist. However, at age fifty-six he experienced an epiphany and entered the spiritual phase of his life. In this new phase, he experienced visions of the spiritual world and claimed to have talked with angels, devils, and spirits and visiting heaven and hell. He claimed that he received direction from God and the Lord Jesus Christ to reveal the doctrine of Christ's Second Coming.

From 1747 until his death in 1772, Swedenborg lived in Stockholm, Holland and London. During these 25 years, he wrote 14 works on spirituality, publishing them during his lifetime. Throughout this period, many people regarded him as a kind and warm-hearted man and befriended him. Some did not believe in his visions. Based on what they had heard, they drew the conclusion that he had lost his mind or had a vivid imagination. Nevertheless, they did not ridicule him in his presence. Those who talked with him understood that he was devoted to his beliefs. He never argued matters of religion, and if obligated to defend himself, he usually did it with gentleness and in a few words.

The Fox Sisters Catherine (1838–92), Leah (1814–90) and Margaret (1836–93) Fox played an important role in the development of Spiritism. The daughters of David and Margaret Fox, they were residents of Hydesville, New York. In 1848, the family began to hear unexplained rapping sounds. Kate and Margaret conducted channeling sessions in an attempt to contact the presumed spiritual entity creating the sounds. The three young women claimed to be in contact with the spirit of a peddler who was allegedly murdered and buried beneath their house. A skeleton discovered weeks later in the basement, seemed to confirm this. The Fox girls became instant celebrities. They demonstrated their communication with spirits by using raps and knocks, automatic writing, and later even voice communication, as the spirit took control of one of the girls.

Skeptics suspected this was nothing but clever deception and fraud. Indeed, sister Margaret eventually confessed to using her toe-joints to produce the sound. Although she later recanted this confession, both she and her sister Catherine were discredited, dying in abject poverty. Nonetheless, belief in the ability to communicate with the dead grew rapidly, becoming a religious movement called Spiritism.

"Talking Boards" Just after the news of the Fox affair came to France; people became even more interested in what became known the "Spiritual Telegraph". Answers to questions appeared as a table spun by means of "energy" produced by spirits. Human channels worked in conjunction with the spirits to facilitate the process. Thus, the term "medium" became

popular. People looked for a new method of communication, because this process was too slow and cumbersome. This suggestion was supposedly made by the spirits themselves using the talking boards.

"People became even more interested in what became known the 'Spiritual Telegraph'".

One example of a talking board was baskets with a pointy object. The object spun under the hands of the medium, to point at letters printed on cards scattered around, or engraved on the table. These devices were called *corbeille à bec* ("basket with a beak"). The pointy object was usually a pencil.

Talking boards were tricky to set up and operate. A typical séance using a talking board saw people sitting at a round table with their feet resting on the chair's supports. Their hands rested on the tabletop or on the talking board itself. The energy channeled from the spirits through their hands made the board spin around and find letters. Once written down by a scribe, these letters would form intelligible words, phrases, and sentences. The method was an early, and less effective forerunner of the Ouija boards that later became so popular.

Allan Kardec first became interested in Spiritism when he learned about the Fox sisters. His first contact with what would become his ideas was by using talking boards. He channeled some of the earlier parts of his *Spirits Book* in this way.[33]

THE FATHER OF SPIRITISM

Allan Kardec was the pen name of Hippolyte Leon Denizard Rivail. He was born in Lyon, France on October 3, 1804. He became a professor and was involved in public education. He wrote books on mathematics and French grammar. As a professor, he taught all subjects, especially the sciences. He spoke six languages fluently. Kardec opened his own school in 1825. In 1831, he married Amelie Gabrielle Boudet, who was also a teacher. Although the couple loved children, they never had a family.

In the mid 1800's in America and Europe, a phenomenon called "table rapping" became a new sensation that eventually developed into an outpouring of important spirit communications. A friend encouraged

---

[33]   Doyle, Sir Arthur Canon. *The History of Spiritualism*. New York: G.H. Doran, Co. 1926

Kardec to attend a séance where he became enamored with the practice of contacting spirits. When convinced of the reality of the spirit world, he devoted his entire life to studying spirit communications. Kardec established the Parisian Society of Psychological Studies and was its president until his death. His group, plus other similar societies throughout Europe, received considerable information from the spirit world. Although he is credited with being the Father of Spiritism, Kardec himself never claimed to be a medium.

Kardec coined the word "Spiritism" in *The Spirits Book* in 1857. He used the word to define Spiritism as a religion. Spiritism, according to Allan Kardec, is a philosophical doctrine with moral implications. However, because the moral implications of Spiritism are similar to the teachings of Jesus Christ and the ethical values of Christianity in general, many Spiritists consider themselves Christians. Kardec believed the message of Spiritism offered love to all human beings, of all cultures, all religious beliefs, and all denominations.

THE INFLUENCE OF SPIRITISM

Spiritism celebrates its birth date on March 31, 1848. It was on this date that Kardec conducted his first American séance with many famous personalities present. The roster of those interested in Spiritism is impressive. Spiritist and renowned physician, Dr. Marcus Bach lists several well-known names interested in psychic phenomena and research. These include celebrities such as James Fennimore Cooper, Daniel Webster, Harriet Beecher Stowe, Elizabeth Barret Browning, Sir Arthur Conan Doyle and Sir William Crooks. Crook's education is impeccable. He held degrees from at least five English universities and was the discoverer of Valium. According to Bach, Crooks reported that he had seen manifestations of levitation and heard accordions play untouched by human hands. He reported seeing luminous handwriting on the wall, and observed a medium handle live coals with her bare hands. He subjected all of this to scientific tests to prove there were forces at work that were inexplicable by any known physical law. Spiritism has a tremendous appeal to the minds of many people as Dr. Bach points out, it confirms for them life after death and reunion with their loved ones.

"Spiritism has a tremendous appeal to the minds of many people, it confirms for them life after death and reunion with their loved ones".

Today the National Spiritualist Association of Churches in the United States reports 54 congregations, with a total membership of about 7,500 people. This does not account for Spiritism's growth in Europe, which reputes to have a much greater membership than in the United States. In South America, there are more than 50 million practicing spiritists, 15 million of these in Brazil alone. This clearly indicates that Spiritism is finding new life, even in what we refer to as the Information Age.[34]

DOCTRINES OF SPIRITISM

The basic teaching of Spiritism, "the Codification", appears in five books written and published by Allan Kardec during his lifetime:

1. *The Spirits Book* — Defines the guidelines of his doctrines, covering points like God, Spirit, Universe, Man, Society, Culture, Morals and Religion.

2. *The Medium's Book* — Details the "mechanics" of the spiritual world, the processes involved in channeling spirits, and techniques to be developed by mediums.

3. *The Gospel According to Spiritism* — Comments on the Gospels, highlight passages that according to Kardec, illustrate the ethical fundamentals shared by all religious and philosophical systems. This may be the first religious book to acknowledge the existence of life elsewhere in the Universe, based on Jesus' saying, "*In My Father's house are many mansions*" (John14: 1-3).

4. *Heaven and Hell* — A didactic series of interviews with spirits of deceased people intending to establish a correlation between the lives they led and their conditions in the beyond.

5. *The Genesis According to Spiritism* — Tries to reconcile religion and science, dealing with the three major points of friction between the two: the origin of the universe, of life, and the concepts of miracles and premonitions.

---

[34] Martin, Walter. *Kingdom of the Cults,* Bethany House publishers, Minneapolis Minnesota, 2003, p. 261.

The following are the fundamental doctrines of Spiritism as delineated by Allan Kardec in his seminal work *The Spirits Book*:

1. There is a God, defined as "The Supreme Intelligence and Primary Cause of everything";

2. There are spirits, all of whom are created simple and ignorant, but owning the power to gradually perfect themselves;

3. The natural method of this perfecting process is reincarnation. Through reincarnation, spirits face countless situations, problems and obstacles, and needs to learn how to deal with them;

4. As part of nature, spirits can naturally communicate with living people, as well as interact with their lives;

5. There are many inhabited planets in the universe.

According to Kardec, spirits desire to contact humanity but need a *channel* through which they can operate. The communication between the spiritual world and the material happens all the time, but to varying degrees. Some people barely sense what the spirits tell them, while others have greater cognizance of their guidance. Mediums have highly developed natural abilities and are able to communicate and interact with the spirits in several ways: listening, seeing, or automatic writing.[35]

SPIRITIST PRACTICES

Séances

One facet of Spiritist practice is to conduct séances. Séances try to communicate with spirits or the deceased. Individuals in the circle have a desire to contact departed loved ones and hope the medium will be able to channel them. The goal is to provide information about the deceased's well-being following death. Well-known Spiritist, John Edwards, hosts a

---

[35]　Kardec, Allan. 2003. *The Gospel Explained by the Spiritist Doctrine.* 2nd Ed. Philadelphia, PA: Allan Kardec Educational Society.

television program called *Crossings*. This program uses spirit contact to reach out to the studio audience.

Clairvoyance

The term Clairvoyance comes from 17th century French word *clair* meaning "clear" and *voyance* meaning "vision". It refers to the ability to see information about an object, person, location or physical event other than with the human senses. Clairvoyance is a form of extra-sensory perception. A person said to have the gift of clairvoyance is "one who sees clearly".

Claims for the existence of paranormal and psychic abilities such as clairvoyance are highly controversial. Parapsychology explores possible psychic abilities, but the scientific community does not accept the existence of the paranormal.

Clairsentience

In the field of parapsychology, Clairsentience is a form of extra-sensory perception where an individual acquires psychic knowledge primarily by means of touch. The word is from the Latin *clarus*, "clear," and *sentiens*, "to feel".

In addition to parapsychology, the term also plays a role in some religions. For example, clairsentience is one of the six special human functions recorded in Buddhism. Spiritists believe that this ability originates during advanced meditation levels. Generally, the term refers to a person who can feel the vibration of other people. There are many different degrees of clairsentience ranging from the perception of diseases in the sick to the ability to read thoughts or emotions in others.

Clairaudience

In the field of parapsychology, Clairaudience, from late 17th century French *clair* (clear) and *audience* (hearing), is a form of extra-sensory perception in which a person acquires paranormal information by auditory means. Clairaudience is the ability to hear the paranormal. It may not necessarily refer to actual perception of sound, but can indicate acquiring impressions of the "inner mental ear". It can also refer to the actual perception of sounds such as voices, tones, or noises that are not apparent to other people or even to recording equipment. For instance, a clairaudient person might claim to hear the voices or thoughts of the spirits of persons who are deceased.

Claircognizance

In the field of parapsychology, Claircognizance, from late 17th century French *clair* (clear) and *cognizance* (thought), is a form of extra-sensory perception in which a person acquires psychic knowledge by means of intrinsic knowing. It is the ability to know something without explanation.

Subtle Bodies

According to various esoteric, occult, and mystical teachings, living beings are comprised of a series of psycho-spiritual bodies called auras. Each aura corresponds to a subtle plane of existence. Subtle bodies exist in a hierarchy or chain of being, that culminates in the physical form.

Subtle bodies are identified in different spiritual traditions as "the most sacred body" or "supra-celestial body." In Sufism, it is "the diamond body," in Taoism and Vajrayana, "the light body" or "rainbow body," in Tibetan Buddhism, "the body of bliss" and in Yoga" the immortal body".

Clairvoyants say that they can see the subtle bodies as an *aura*. The practice of astral projection, as described in various literatures, is supposed to involve the separation of the subtle body from the physical. The Theosophical movement was important in spreading such ideas throughout the West in the late nineteenth century.

Astral Projection

Astral travel is a type of out-of-body experience. It assumes the existence of an "astral body," separate from the physical body, and capable of traveling outside it. Unlike dreaming or near death experiences, astral projection takes place deliberately and sometimes occurs spontaneously.

Psychokinesis

The term psychokinesis, from "psyche", meaning *mind,* and, "kinesis", meaning *"movement from the mind,"* is also called as telekinesis, literally "distant-movement". At times, they are abbreviated as PK and TK respectively. Psychokinesis is a term coined by publisher Henry Holt to refer to the ability of the mind to move objects without any known physical energy.

Telepathy

Telepathy means "*distant knowledge*," refers to the transference of information, thoughts, or feelings between individuals by means other than the five senses. The term originated in 1882 by the classical scholar Fredric W. H. Myers, a founder of the Society for Psychical Research. He used telepathy specifically to replace the earlier expression *thought-transference*. A person who is able to use telepathy can read the thoughts and stored information in the minds of others. Telepathy, along with psychokinesis forms the main branches of para-psychological research. Many studies seeking to detect, understand, and utilize telepathy have been done within the field.

Channeling

Channeling is a state that exists when a medium falls into a trance. At this time, they "leave their body" and become "possessed" by a spirit who talks through them. In the trance, the medium enters a cataleptic state marked by extreme rigidity. The control spirit then takes over. The voice may change completely and the spirit answers the questions of those in its presence or voluntarily gives spiritual knowledge.

The most successful and widely known channeler of this variety is J. Z. Knight, who claims to channel the spirit of Ramtha, a 30 thousand year old man. Some claim to channel spirits from "future dimensional planes", Ascended Masters, or in the case of some trance mediums, God himself. Channeling is a popular parody in the "*Doonesbury*" cartoon where a ditzy female character channels "Hunk-Ra," an assertive 21,000-year-old warrior.

Spirit Guides

A spirit guide is a highly evolved spirit whose sole purpose is helping the medium develop and use their skills. Mediums claim that these guides assist them in following their spiritual path. Other mediums claim a spirit guide is one who brings other spirits to a medium's attention or carries communications between the medium and the spirits of the dead. Many mediums have specific guides who regularly work with them and "bring in" spirits of the deceased. Some mediums claim that spirits of the dead will communicate with them directly without the use of a spirit guide.[36]

---

36   Tanner, Amy. 1994, *Studies in Spiritism*, Prometheus Press, page 18.

A CAREFUL RECORD OF A SÉANCE

It is invaluable to include a record of an actual séance to have a full understanding of the practice of Spiritism. One such example is that of Dr. Marcus Bach, noted English physician. He examined many instances of spiritualistic phenomena in an effort to discredit the movement. Instead, Dr. Bach eventually became an ardent believer in Spiritism and one it's most prominent proponents. Bach kept a detailed record of one particularly convincing séance that he attended.

"Suddenly the galaxy of spirits melted away".

The record of this account is included here by courtesy of the late Dr. Walter Martin, one of the foremost authorities on cults and the occult. Dr. Bach describes the séance in the following way:

"I was making minute mental notations of all that was happening--the hovering, swaying motion of the spiritists, the rhythm of life, like the rise and fall of a tie, as many as four speaking simultaneously in whispered voices, excited, hurried persuasive. Suddenly the galaxy of spirits melted away. For long still moments, nothing happened. Then the swirling ectoplasmic effluvia glowed from the floor and quickly took on the form of a girl. Before the figure was complete, it spoke.

"Marc, dear-Marc, dear-Marc, dear."

Those who know me well call me Marc; those who know me more closely call me 'Marc, dear', so I knew this must be a familiar spirit! I got up and walked over until there was a space of less than four feet between us. "Yes I said who are you?" The answer was fraught with disappointment.

"Don't you know me?"

I did not. I had no idea who this might be. I had really been much to absorbed to think very much about personal contact with the spirits. Nor did I propose to offer any hints of whom I thought she might represent. No leads, I determined.

"I do not know you. Who are you?"

"Paula," came the soft answer.

Twenty years ago my sister Paula had died at the age of 23. Her child Janette had died shortly before. These deaths had been among the deepest sorrows of our family, but time and travel reduced the past into forgetfulness. No medium or spirit had plucked this name out of my mind because I wasn't thinking of Paula. I had not thought of her even once during the séance. I looked at the presence before me closely.

"How do I look?" she asked.

"You look fine," I replied.

"Right height?" she whispered.

"Do you think I should be taller?"

"No. You are about the right height I remember."

"I wanted to do a good job," she told me earnestly. "Do I look all right?"

"Yes, I assured her." Materialization occurs when the spirit takes the ectoplasmic form according to the memory of those present. Did this form in these features resemble Paula? I must admit it did very much. The outline of the figure was recognizable and convincing. It was like a false front, a flat, two-dimensional body with a semblance of arms, clothes, and a shadowy gray white film. The face itself was masklike. There was no illusion of long blond hair. I cannot say whether the voice was Paula's or not. After 20 years, I would not remember. Just now, however, it was Paula returned.

Nevertheless, why shouldn't it be, I asked myself as I stood there. The spiritualists at Chesterfield knew I was coming. If, as some people say, they have a well-laid system of espionage, they could easily have traced my family and matched Paula's description. If this was someone dressed up, play acting or if this was a marionette using the voice of a ventriloquist; naturally it would be constructed to represent Paula. This thought haunted me more than the presence. I wished I could convince myself some way. The impulse to reach out and touch the figure became stronger. I moved closer. I moved slightly to one side so that the red light would strike the spirit's face more directly. We were about 3 feet apart now. Paula was talking about life in the Spirit world. I was asking hasty questions: "Have you seen Jesus"? "What is heaven really like"? "What about the element of time"? "Can you be everywhere at once"? "Are terms like Methodist, Reformed, Presbyterian, and Catholic ever used where you are"?

Her voice seemed to laugh. She answered no to all questions save the one about heaven. It was like speaking to a living person secretly, clandestinely, knowing that time was running out. Her features seem to become clearer. Perhaps it was my mind playing tricks.

Another thought came to me. "Paula," I said, "do you remember the catechism we learned at home?"

"Of course!"

"Paula, do you remember the first question in the catechism?"

"I remember."

"What was it?" I asked that almost fearfully.

The answer came at once, "What is your chief comfort in life and in death?"

"Go on," I urged.

"That both in life and in death I am not my own."

She interrupted herself. "Here words have greater significance and meaning!"

Then quickly, breathlessly, she told me that, "serving God means personal development. Life on the spirit plane is involvement, like the breaking of a chrysalis. Like the growth of moral affection to higher and higher levels."

Several times, she interrupted herself with, "Do you understand?" "Is that clear?" She spoke as if she felt her message was vital and all absorbing. Death, she insisted, was not a violent result of sin. It had no sting. It was neither friend nor enemy. It was part of the divine purpose, a purpose without beginning or end".

The whispering grew fainter. "I can no longer stay. I must go now."

"Paula, one more thing, can you put your arms around me?"

"I'll give you a kiss", she said. "Come closer."

"You come close to me." I wanted her to come nearer the red light. Her face was luminous, seemingly transparent, and without depth. I leaned forward and lowered my head. The web like texture of ectoplasmic arms encircled my neck. Something soft and flaxen brushed my forehead. Then Paula vanished into the floor it seemed. I walked back to my chair and sat down and the séance was over.[37]

After seeing this manifestation of his sister Paula, Marcus Bach became convinced in the idea of the existence of life after death. However, his belief did not rest in the resurrection of Jesus Christ as the first fruits from the dead, but in the counterfeit trappings of Spiritism.

As Christians, we know that Dr. Bach did not make contact with his deceased sister but was in fact communicating with a demonic imitation of her. The dead cannot communicate with the living. As the Bible states, "*There is a vast gulf fixed between us*" (Luke 16:26). Unfortunately, the master of deception fooled Dr. Bach and thwarted him from the truth. Jesus said, "*I am the Way, the Truth and the Life no man comes to the Father but by me*" (John 14:26).

SPIRITISM AND TOUCH THERAPIES

Touch Therapies have a great deal in common with the practice of Spiritism. Many of its proponents openly admit to using spiritistic methods in their therapeutic modalities. The founder of one popular touch therapy freely admits that she is, "the fourteenth generation of clairvoyants in her family able to read *auras* to induce healing". Still others claim to use telepathy to communicate with their clients. Others use clairaudience to listen for instructions and gain insight to aid in healing. Most practice channeling to ascertain the help of spirit guides to assist them in their "psychic treatments".

---

[37] Martin, Walter. *Kingdom of the Cults*, Bethany House publishers, Minneapolis Minnesota. 2003. p. 270-272. *Used by permission. (Jill Martin Rische)*

*"Many choose to participate in the occult with their
eyes wide open, understanding the depths of evil
it represents".*

These demonstrate but a few ways in which touch therapies use occult mechanisms in their practice of healing. Satan's lies seduce them like Dr. Bach was. The Bible warns us, *"Be not deceived, God is not mocked. For whatsoever a man sows, that shall he also reap."* (Galatians 6:7). On the other hand, not all are deceived. Many choose to participate in the occult with their eyes wide open, understanding the depths of evil it represents. They have knowingly exchanged the *"truth of God for a lie and served the creature more than the Creator, who is blessed forever. Amen"* (Roman 1:25).

God's Word expressly condemns such practices repeatedly, even if it is for the benefit of "medicine" and "wellness". In Deuteronomy 18:9-11 the Bible records God's commands to His people to reject the ways of the nations around them. He issues a stern injunction prohibiting Israel from practicing the occult abominations of the Canaanites. He admonishes them saying, *"When you enter the land the LORD your God is giving you, do not learn to imitate the detestable ways of the nations there. Let no one be found among you who sacrifices his son or daughter in the fire, who practices divination or sorcery, interprets omens, engages in witchcraft, or casts spells, or who is a medium or spiritist or who consults the dead."* This injunction remains in effect for us today.

A NEW JUNCTURE

It is very exciting to come to this point in writing because we are about to examine three touch therapies and discover how they appropriate the religious and occult practices that have been discussed so far. Many people are greatly surprised to learn how religious and occult ideas are masquerading as touch therapies and worming their way into our medical system.

STUDY QUESTIONS

THE EVILS OF SPIRITISM

1. What do we mean when we use the phrase, "the occult"?

2. Why were the Fox sisters so well-known?

3. From what device was the modern Ouija Board modeled on? What was its purpose and how did it work? Why are Ouija Boards spiritually dangerous?

4. Who was Allan Kardec and what his influence on the development of Spiritism?

5. What are the five fundamental doctrines of Spiritism?

6. Name and define Spiritists major practices.

7. What spiritist practices do you see incorporated in Dr. Bach's record of a séance?

8. What practices do Spiritism and Touch Therapies share?

9. What does the Bible say about Spiritism?

CHAPTER 6

SPIRITUAL HEALING THOUGH REIKI

CHAPTER 6
SPIRITUAL HEALING THOUGH REIKI

*"Lay hands suddenly on no man, neither be
partaker of other men's sins: keep thyself pure".*
— 1 Timothy 5:2

The majority of people have never heard of the term "Reiki". Nonetheless, this alternative therapy is currently being practiced in 15% of U. S. hospitals. It is also used in a larger segment of hospice programs.[38] This translates into multiple thousands of people using Reiki. Reiki is consistently gaining popularity as an alternative therapy. More medical continuing education programs offer Reiki as a part of their curriculum. Still, a majority of the public is not familiar with Reiki so it is necessary to help them learn about it. Reki is infiltrating our medical system at an alarming rate. It will not be long until Christian professionals and their patients encounter it.

Reiki is a Japanese word meaning *"universal life energy"*. In Japanese, Reiki is represented by two *kanji*, or pictograms. The first pictogram, *Rei*, means *"universal transcendent spirit"* or *"boundless essence"*. The second pictogram, *Ki,* translates as the" *life force energy"*. This "life force energy" is the energy that resides in all created matter: animal, vegetable, and mineral. Reiki is a simple technique for transferring healing energy from a therapist to a client. A practitioner receives the ability to heal through Reiki *attunements* during special initiation ceremonies. The attunement opens a channel in the initiate for the universal life energy to flow through. Thus, healing occurs on a physical, mental, emotional, or spiritual level.

---

[38] https://iarp.org/reiki-clinical-setting/ (Accessed December 3, 2022).

The attunements during First, Second, and Third Degree seminars, are by a certified Master Reiki Teacher. The unique *Reiki symbols* with their *mantras,* enable Reiki energy to work on a vibrational level. These symbols are passed from Reiki Master to the student in secret, during the Second and Third Degree initiations. As secret symbols, they are kept inviolate.

Reiki traces its roots directly to Buddhism and a 19th Century monk named Dr. Mikao Usui. Inherent in its practice, are the pantheistic teachings of Buddhism's concept of "all is god, and god is all". Since the Universal Life Force encompasses all things, animate and inanimate, it pervades everything from the ground we walk on, to the air we breathe.

To clarify what Reiki is even further, Reiki Master Bill Waites writes, "*Rei,* is the infinite higher intelligence which guides the creation and functioning of the universe and is the source guide in our lives. It is the wisdom of God, or the High Power, or God-consciousness. Reiki is supernatural knowledge and spiritual consciousness. It understands and knows each person completely, as it is omniscient and omnipresent. *Rei*ki knows the cause of all problems and difficulties, and understands how to heal them.

Ki, is the life force energy that animates everything. It gives life and is the Vital Life Force that flows through us via the *chakras* and *meridians*. *Ki* is found all around us and is responsible for creating the auric body ".[39] It is easy to see how Reiki philosophy incorporates Buddhist teaching.

DR. MIKAO USUI FOUNDER OF REIKI

Reiki has a very interesting history. Its is the story of an apostate Christian college professor who after a long search returned to his Buddhist roots to find a method of healing. Dr. Usui lived in the city of Kyodo, Japan in the second half of the 19th Century. This was a time of great change in Japan. The country had recently open to foreigners and the influx of Christian missionaries. Dr. Usui was originally a follower of Shintoism and Buddha in the Japanese style. Later, he embraced Christianity, and became a minister as well as a teacher at a Christian Bible College for men in Kyoto. During one of his classes, some students asked him if he literally believed in the Bible. Dr. Usui replied that he did. His students then asked him

---

39   Waites, Bill. (1998). *Reiki: A Practical Guide.* Hod Hasharon, Israel: Astrolog Publishing House. p. 124.

how he explained the miraculous healings of Jesus and His instructions to the apostles to heal the sick and raise the dead. They also asked him what Jesus meant when he said, "you will go and do as I have done and even greater things". If this were true, they reasoned with Dr. Usui, the world should be full of healers.

"Reiki is based on Buddhist teaching".

Dr. Usui had no reply for his students, but felt personally challenged to go out and find the answer. Usui resigned his position at the college in order to discover the way in which Jesus healed the sick. Because Western missionaries had taught him that Christianity is a Western religion, he decided that the West was where he should look for his answers. He travelled to the United States where he lived for seven years. Usui enrolled at a theological seminary in Chicago and studied comparative religions. It was there that he learned to read Sanskrit. Sanskrit is the ancient language of India and Tibet, and the language of many religious texts. He did not find the answers he sought in his studies so he decided to return to Japan. Usui also decided to return to his Buddhist roots thinking that the Japanese Lotus Sutra contained information about the healing method used by the Buddha.

Dr. Usui traveled to many Buddhist monasteries asking the monks if they had information about the Buddha's method of healing. Although the sutras record that the Buddha performed healing, the practice of Buddhism had shifted entirely to healing the spirit. As a result, none of the monks that Dr. Usui encountered could help him.

Finally, Usui approached a Zen monastery where the Abbott agreed with him that it is possible to heal the body as the Buddha had done. However, during the centuries of concentration on healing the spirit, the method had been lost.

Greatly encouraged, Dr. Usui stayed at the monastery where he studied the Japanese Buddhist Sutras in the original Sanskrit. Although he found the text that described a method of healing, he still lacked the information that would enable him to activate the energy and use it himself. Dr. Usui concluded that he might gain more information if he traveled to Tibet and studied the Tibetan Buddhist Sutras. In the 19th Century, archaeologists discovered scrolls in Tibet that documented the travels of a great healer throughout the Himalayas who many thought was Jesus. There is no evidence that Dr. Usui read the scrolls. However, after he completed his study of the Tibetan Buddhist Sutras, he felt he had found the intellectual answers he longed for but, still could not activate the healing energy. Usui returned to the Zen monastery and after discussing his dilemma with the Abbott, decided that he should go on a 21-day retreat to fast and meditate.

The place Dr. Usui and the Abbott chose for the retreat was Mount Kuri Yama, a sacred mountain not far from Kyoto. Climbing the eastern face of the mountain, Dr. Usui collected 21 stones in a pile to serve as his calendar. He intended to throw away a stone at the end of every day to tell time. Just before dawn on his 21st day, there was the new moon and it was very dark. As he felt for the last stone, he prayed for an answer to come. At that moment, he saw a light hurtling towards him from across the sky. As it got closer to him, it became larger and larger. At first he was afraid, and wanted to run away from it. Nevertheless, he decided to accept whatever it would bring him, even if it was death. As he faced it, the light struck him in the third eye (the sixth chakra) in the center of his forehead. Millions of rainbow colored bubbles appeared before his eyes and he saw the Reiki symbols. As he viewed the symbols, he received information about each one and its use in activating the healing energy. At that moment, Buddha's healing method incarnated in the form of Reiki.

When Dr. Usui came out of his trance like state, he found it was broad daylight. He started to run down the mountain to share his discovery. As he ran toward the Zen monastery, he tripped on a stone and stubbed his toe. He bent down to hold his toe and was amazed when after a few minutes, the bleeding stopped and the toe was completely healed. This was the first miracle.

Now Dr. Usui had to decide how to use the new found power. After meditation and consultation with the Abbott, he chose to work in the Beggar's Quarter of Kyoto. He healed many people, but found that many of the ones he healed returned to begging. He asked one man why he had done so. The man explained that following his healing he found a job and was married. However, he could not handle being responsible for his own life, and so he preferred to be a beggar.

Discouraged by this attitude, Dr. Usui left the Beggar's Quarter and traveled throughout Japan teaching Reiki. He discovered that he could use the Reiki symbols to attune others so that they could also give Reiki and take responsibility for their own lives. As a result, he started to train other men as Reiki Masters. One of these men was Chujiro Hayashi. Hayashi became Dr. Usui's successor and responsible for carrying on the traditions of Reiki.

Interestingly, there is no evidence that Usui discovered the merits of Christianity in the United States. Perhaps he was always a Buddhist, but he added the Christian concept of healing to his practice of Reiki. Until his death, Usui claimed that if Jesus healed the sick, then Reiki must be okay. It is also interesting to note that there is no record of Usui teaching at Doshiba University or ever attending the seminary at the University of Chicago. Finally, there is no legal record of him earning a doctorate, either scholastically or medically. Perhaps it was an honorary title given to him later in life by his Reiki students, perhaps not.

DR. CHUJIRO HAYASHI AND MRS. HAWAYO TAKATA

Dr. Hayashi was a retired naval officer who followed Dr. Usui's teachings and founded a Reiki clinic in Tokyo. Here he trained many in the use of Reiki. In his clinic, healers worked with sick people and went to their homes if they were not able to come to the clinic. Not Dr. Hayashi remains somewhat of an enigma, although new material coming out of Japan suggests that like Dr. Usui, he created many Reiki Masters. His spiritual or psychic abilities were critical to the survival of Reiki. One of the visitors to his clinic was Mrs. Takata who came to be cured.

Hawayo Takata was born in 1900 on the Hawaiian island of Kauai. In 1935, she developed a nervous exhaustion accompanied by an illness and was told that she required surgery to save her life. While on a visit to Japan to see her parents, she went to a hospital for the surgery. On the day of the operation, as she prepared for the anesthetic, she heard a voice tell her, "The operation is unnecessary". She spoke to her doctor about her reservations and asked him if there was another way to avoid surgery. The doctor said that he knew of a place in Tokyo where she could go to if she was able to stay in Japan for a longer period of time. The doctor was familiar with Reiki because his sister had been healed and had become a practitioner. When Mrs. Takata arrived at Dr. Hayashi's Reiki clinic, she received treatment and cured.

"She heard a voice tell her, 'The operation is unnecessary'".

After staying at the clinic for some months, she asked Dr. Hayashi if he would teach her Reiki. At first, he refused because she was a foreigner and he was concerned about Reiki leaving Japan. However, Hayashi eventually approved and initiated Mrs. Takata in the First and Second Degrees before returning to Hawaii where she began her own practice. In 1938, about a year after she had gone back to Hawaii, Dr. Hayashi visited Mrs. Takata, and initiated her as a Reiki Master. He later announced that she was to be his successor and was responsible for carrying on the traditions of Reiki. He also told her that whenever he summoned her to Japan she must come immediately.

Dr. Hayashi had powerful psychic abilities and foresaw that Japan and America were going to war against each other in the near future. He also knew the war would be not fare well for Japan. He sent for Mrs. Takata to come to Tokyo. When she arrived, he shared his vision with her and told her what she must do to preserve Reiki. As he had previously been a naval officer, he was afraid that he would be drafted into military service, which was now against his principles. Later, in full ceremonial dress, and with all his family and friends around him, Dr. Hayashi consciously left his body.

Mrs. Takata returned to Hawaii and somehow managed to escape incarceration as a Japanese-American during the war. After the war, she brought Reiki to mainland America. During the last 10 years of her life (she died on December 11, 1980), she initiated 22 Reiki Masters who spread Reiki throughout America, Europe and the rest of the world. She also named her granddaughter, Phyllis Furumoto as her successor. Many Reiki Masters recognize Mrs. Furumoto as the Grandmaster of the movement.[40]

WESTERN REIKI

Since Mrs. Takata brought Reiki to the United States, several schools of Reiki healing have developed. There is the school of *Usui Shiki Ryoho,* as taught by Hayashi and Takata; *Usui Reiki Ryoho,* the system taught today in Japan; and *Usui Tibetan Reiki,* which incorporates Tibetan Symbols.

---

[40]   McKenzie, Eleanor. *Healing Reiki,* Ulysses Press, Berkley, CA 1998 p. 46-49

The Radiance Technique taught by Barbara Ray claims that Mrs. Takata gave her "all" the attunements in a six level system. *Seichim*, taught by Patrick Zeiler, combines Reiki with Egyptian mysticism. David Jarrell (1946–2002), was the founder of *Reiki Plus*. Students who complete the First and Second Degrees of Reiki Plus can apply for ordination as ministers in the Pyramids of Light Church.

Wei Chi Tibetan Reiki is allegedly based on the teachings of Wei Chi, a 5,000-year-old Tibetan monk. Kevin Ross Emery channeled Wei Chi in his bathtub one night in 1995 in the presence of his partner, Tommy Hensel. *Lightarian Reiki* is another branch of the technique, created in 1997 by Reiki and Karuna master Jeanine Marie Jelm. Jelm claims to have channeled information from the ascended master Buddha. The list of traditions continues to grow, each with its own distinctives and practices.

Reiki practitioners in the West also have strong ties to the occult. These include *Elisabeth Jensen R.N.* Therapeutic Touch Teacher, Past, Parallel and Future Lives Therapist, Certified Angel Intuitive Practitioner, Crystal Healer, Aura Reading and Healing Therapist, Past Life Regression Therapist, Reiki Master, Certified Hypnotist and Certified Angel Therapist Practitioner.

Barbra Brennan, PhD. She holds a ThD in healing and is the founder of the Brennan School of Healing. She grants degrees in Healing Science, Hands-on Energy Healing, and Transformation. Included in her books are instructions for contacting spirit guides and angels. Brennan specializes in teaching her concepts to nurses.

Dora Kunz, co-founder of Therapeutic Touch, bases her teaching on the early 20th Century writings of *Charles Leadbeater* (1847-1934). Leadbeater was a clairvoyant and former curate of the Church of England who converted to Buddhism. Kunz directs workshops targeted at professional nurses.[41]

THE REIKI SYMBOLS

The practice of Reiki is powerless outside of the use of the three symbols that Dr. Usui discovered in his vision on Mt. Kuri Yama. Let us briefly examine them.

---

[41] Mooney, Sharon Fish. *Reiki: With Minds Wide Open*, Christian Research Journal, Vol. 29, No. 6 (2006)

Reiki symbols are sacred healing signs that enhance the flow of the Universal Life Energy. They are like keys that open doors to higher levels of awareness and manifestation. The Reiki symbols taught during the Second Degree and Masters training are an essential aspect of Reiki. These symbols differentiate Reiki from other healing methods and are used to introduce the esoteric and occult.

Reiki symbols derive from a Japanese variation of Sanskrit. Advocates say that Sanskrit is the mother tongue of all other languages. It is the language of the Vedas, the oldest writings known to man. The Vedas state that Sanskrit is *the language of the spirit world.*

Students receive the Reiki symbols during attunement. When revealed, an imprinting takes place that links the images to the metaphysical energies the symbols represent. The Reiki attunement actually empowers the symbols so that they fulfill their intended purpose. This process creates a divine covenant or sacred agreement between the Creator and the recipient.

The symbols have their own consciousness, and it is possible to meditate on them and receive guidance on how to use them directly from the symbols themselves.

EXPLANATION OF THE SYMBOLS

Cho Ku Rei This is the Power Symbol. Reiki Energy will flow without it, but when in used, the energy increases significantly. It is as if you had changed the bulb in a lamp from 50 watts to 500 watts. This symbol is part of the beginning of the healing session, and at any other time, that additional power is needed. This symbol works specifically for healing the physical body. Traditionally the symbol means, "Put the power here" or "god is here" It is the symbol used in the first level of attunement.

Sei He Ki This symbol is part of mental and emotional healing, protection, purification, clearing and balancing. The symbol means, "Man and God becoming one". It is used to bring balance to the mind and emotions. This single symbol is very powerful. It heals anger, depression, sadness, fear, and addictions. It also deals with any difficult feelings or thoughts. Sei He Ki is the symbol used in the second attunement.

"The essential message of the symbol is 'The Buddha in me greets the Buddha in you'".

Hon Sha Ze Sho Nen Tlike This symbol heals beyond space and time, working on all levels and dimensions. This means that you can send Reiki into the "past" to heal previous issues, or to heal past life issues that continue to affect you now. The symbol transmits Reiki energy across time and space. By using this symbol, you can send Reiki across the room, across town, to other parts of the country or anywhere in the world. Distance is no barrier. You can also use this symbol to bridge time and send Reiki into the "future," where it will store up. The essential message of the symbol is "The Buddha in me greets the Buddha in you." This symbol is also part of the Second Degree attunement.

Dai Ko Myo This is the Master Symbol. It translates as the "Light of the Buddha, the Light of the Awakened Heart". It signifies expanded wisdom and clairvoyance. This symbol is used for the healing of the soul, the level of the blueprint from which the physical body is derived. This symbol means, "Great Being of the universe, shine on me, be my friend". It is primarily part of attunements to connect the recipient to the Reiki energy and the higher self.

As said earlier, the symbols themselves are secret and not disclosed to anyone other than a Reiki Master who is qualified to make the attunements. Nevertheless, these symbols have been obtained through those who have left the movement.[42]

HOW REIKI SYMBOLS FUNCTION

In ancient times, Tibetan monks recognized that healing channels could be set to vibrate in order to transfer more energy. The Symbols and *"mantras"* used in Reiki increase the vibrational frequency of the whole body.

The symbol itself comprises a pictorial drawing also known as a mantra. The drawing depicts a visual representation while the name allows you to hear its sound and experience its vibration. The repetition of the mantra is internal and never spoken aloud. The practitioner works non-verbally on a particular wavelength to create the vibration. This is similar in concept to telepathy.

Reiki advocates believe that sound and mantras have the ability to vibrate certain chakras depending on the vibratory level. Through repetition of a mantra, for example *"OM"*, you can activate the upper energy centers.

---

[42]   Usui Reiki Symbols https://www.reiki.org/articles/usui-reiki-symbols (Accessed October 14, 2022).

In the attunement process of the First, Second, and Third Degree, the Reiki Master uses symbols and mantras to create a similar but much higher vibration to channel the Universal Life Energy.

The First Symbol activates the general energy field. This symbol helps re-energize the practitioner and recipient wherever energy is lacking. The Second Symbol adds a quality of harmony, peace, and balance to the etheric body, chakra system, and especially for mental healing. The Third Symbol works on the mental level as it opens up intuition and strengthens the ability to see into the spirit world. It connects to the third eye or sixth chakra and is part of distance healing. It is used when energy and thoughts are sent to people who are absent. The Fourth Symbol or Master Symbol strengthens the ability to open up to higher energies and to become a channel for them. The vibration of this symbol is a very strong force. Reiki Masters use it to channel higher energies during attunements.[43]

THE THREE DEGREES OF REIKI ATTUNEMENTS

Reiki initiations are separated into three degrees, the third being the initiation as Reiki Master. The three degrees include initiation, development, and mastery.

The First Degree From the first attunement, most people feel the energy flowing through their hands. Some people also feel the presence of spirits, while still others see vivid colors or experience intense feelings of love. After a break, the second attunement takes place. At this time, the master will show the hand positions for self-treatment and for treating others. Finally, the last attunement grounds the energy and seals it permanently. It gets rid of the negative energy so that for the rest of your life you will be able to channel the energy even if you do not use it for a long time.

Following the attunements, it is traditional for all students to give themselves Reiki treatments every day for 21 days. This symbolically represents the time Dr. Usui spent fasting and meditating, but is also the amount of time it takes for new energy to move through each of the seven chakras and settle in.

The Second Degree In the Second Degree class, the student receives only one attunement. This opens the chakras further, and allows the student to use

---

[43]   Honervogt, Tanmaya, (1998). *The Power of Reiki: An Ancient Hands-On Healing Technique.* New York: Henry Holt and Company. p. 40

the three symbols that amplify the rate of the energy and facilitates distance healing. Learning and working with the symbols is the key aspect of the Second Degree. The hand positions for treating self and others are elements of First Degree initiation. The Second Degree initiation includes one new hand position that is specifically used for mental and emotional healing. This symbol also enables the student to send *distance healing* to others.

The Third Degree The Third Degree trains the student to become a Reiki Master and teacher. If you are considering taking this step, you should approach a Reiki Master and discuss it with them carefully. Only a Reiki Master may attune students. Within the Usui tradition, Mrs. Takata set the cost of becoming a Reiki Master at $10,000. In Eastern cultures, students of spiritual paths must commit years of their lives to studying with the teacher before they are ready to teach others therefore, the $10,000 is compensation for time.

AN ACCOUNT OF FIRST DEGREE INITIATION

The following is an actual account of a First Degree Reiki Attunement given by a nurse. "Never before had I consciously fallen into states of such deep relaxation as I did during my first attunement. I saw vivid colors and bright lights inside myself, but what most impressed me were the images and memories that put me in contact with past lives. The concept of reincarnation is a commonly accepted truth in Eastern religions and cultures whereby the physical body dies at the end of life and a soul is reborn. The soul reincarnates, repeatedly into another body, until it reaches self-realization or enlightenment. I was overjoyed to discover something that could bring me closer to myself.

> *"I saw vivid colors and bright lights inside myself, but what most impressed me were the images and memories that put me in contact with past lives".*

I remember my initiation into the First Degree. I received my energy and learned the special hand positions. Now I was a Reiki channel. Still somewhat uncertain, I started tentatively to try out what I had learned so far. I distinctly remember giving a Reiki treatment to a woman in my guesthouse. This was an unforgettable moment for me because it was the first time I had ever experienced healing as a giver of hands on treatment. The woman came to me with a bad headache, but felt better after my treatment. The pain in her head dissolved as my hands became hot and tingly. I could actually feel energy drawing into her.[44]

REIKI BELIEFS

As we can see, Reiki is not a medical therapy but is instead a Buddhist belief system. Although it cloaks itself as a healing method, it facilitates Buddhist philosophy. Reiki promotes a belief in the *Universal Life Force*, the *Chakra system*, *Marma points*, and *Meridian Lines*, none of which are scientifically verifiable. Let us take a moment to examine a few of Reiki's key beliefs.

The Universal Life Force As humans, the" *Universal Life Force*" is all around us and within us. The Japanese word Reiki consists of two syllables "*rei*", which describes the "cosmic universal aspect" of this energy, and "*ki*", which means "the fundamental life force flowing and pulsating in all living things". This life force energy is given to us at birth. From birth, we have a certain amount of Reiki life force, and we use it in the business of ordinary daily living. Historically, there are different words for this fundamental force in the various cultures and religions of the world. The Chinese know it as "*qi*", and Hindus use "*prana*". In the West, we call this force, "bio-energy" or" cosmic energy".

The Chakras The Reiki treatment and hand positions correspond to the in endocrine system and coincide with the Hindu concept of seven Chakras. The word "*Chakra*" comes from the Sanskrit meaning "*Wheel*". Chakras are an imaginary energy port or vortex where the universal life energy channels into the body.

Physiologically, the endocrine system regulates hormone balances and metabolism. Reiki believes that the endocrine glands correspond to the seven main Chakras or energy centers. Practitioners develop the occult gift of clairvoyance. With this, they claim to see the Chakras as spinning energy spirals of light, which differ in size and activity from one person to another. They propose that the Chakras are components of the human etheric body. Chakras connect to the energy channels running along the spine. Without them, the physical body could not exist. These chakric

---

[44]　Ibid. p.16

energy centers collect subtle energy, transform it, and supply it to the rest of the body. Each Chakra links to certain organs and regions of the body to induce healing. The Chakra System is as follows:

- The Crown 7th: represents spiritual awareness, intuition, and connection to the Higher Self;
- The Third Eye or forehead 6th: represents clairvoyance, telepathy, inner vision, and spiritual awakening;
- The Throat 5th; represents self-expression, creativity and communication;
- The Heart 4th: represents the center of the emotions: love, peace, sympathy, forgiveness, trust, and compassion;
- Solar Plexus 3rd: represents personal power, dominance, strength and fear;
- Sacral 2nd; represents enjoyment of life, self esteem, feelings, and desire for relationships;
- Root 1st: represents physical health, survival, sexual drive and procreation.

The Meridians The meridians are an Oriental anatomical belief in conduits or channels in the body that conduct "qi" or energy. They are separate from all the other anatomical systems in the body. According to this belief, there are 14 meridians channels, 12 of which are primary.

The Marma Scholars of Chinese and Indian medicine identify marma as energy points that provide contact between the physical body and the astral body, and convey cosmic energy. Along the length of each meridian are minute perforations that carry cosmic energy throughout a person's physical and ethereal body. Marma points supposedly open energy channels throughout the body. There are 52 marma points that form the basis of the entire meridian network and all the acupuncture and massage points used in touch therapy.

The ability of the Reiki expert to open these points is far greater than any other technique. They open the connecting channel, and the Reiki energy flows into the correct place, in the right quantity and potency. In this way, the body and mind are "controlled" through energizing the marma point.[45]

---

45   Ibid, p.22.

The way this works according to proponents of Reiki, is that the practitioner channels the Universal Life Force into the chakra system. It penetrates the specific parts of the body via the marma points, into the meridian lines until the energy connects with the diseased part of the body to produce healing.

Nevertheless, Reiki is more than the direction of an inexplicable Buddhist energy force. Reiki is also an incorporation of spiritual beliefs that integrates occult elements of Buddhism. Celebrated Reiki Master, William Lee Rand, openly admits this very thing. Rand's writings and personal interviews discuss how occult practices, such as telepathic communication with angels and spirit guides is used in Reiki.

Rand writes, "There are higher sources of help you can call on. *Angels, Beings of Light* and *Reiki Spirit Guides* as well as your own *enlightened self* are available to help you. They can help you develop your Reiki practice by directing clients to you and assisting with treatments. They can be of great benefit, but you must have a strong spiritual intention for your work if you are to recruit their aid.

Those who use Reiki in a selfish way, such as for money, to gain control over others, or for any other negative purpose, makes it difficult for *spiritual beings* to work with you. There must be congruence, or an inner alignment in order for the *Higher Power* to flow through you or for the angels, spirit guides and other spiritual beings to work with you".[46]

"There are higher sources of help you can call on".

One must not minimize the use of other occult methods in the practice of Reiki. For instance, Reiki communication comes in many forms. According to Rand, Reiki practitioners receive information differently. Spirits communicate through intuition, sound, touch, voices, color, hunches, déjà vu, thoughts, symbols, visions, dreams, feelings, smells, writing and other creative ways.

The occult ability that Rand uses to hear supernatural messages is *Clairaudience*. Those who are visually oriented, and those with visual psychic skills are called *Clairvoyant*. Still others receive information by simply knowing without a real sense of words or visions. They are *Claircognizant*.

---

[46]   Developing Your Reiki Practice http://www.reiki.org/ReikiPractice/ PracticeHomepage.html (Accessed October 14, 2022)

Those who gain occult insight through touch are *Clairsentient*. Reiki practitioners can have endless variations of all of these occult gifts.

There are those who believe that Reiki gives some therapists a greater awareness of the spirit world. They state that Reiki can free those trapped between worlds without physical bodies (or ghosts), through touch. It is becoming more common to hear about people using Reiki for exorcisms, house protection, cleansing, and banishing unwanted spirits. Their contention is that this is a natural extension of the healing process of Reki.

In addition to these beliefs and practices, Reiki also alleges beliefs in channeling incorporeal spirits and the deceased. They believe in the existence of etheric bodies or auras and build bridges to former lives through past life regression based on reincarnation. Interestingly, Reiki teaches that individuals may influence the past to resolve negative events like family disagreements, or influence future events such as job interviews or surgery.

THE USE OF REIKI IN MEDICINE

According to advocates, Reiki uses the biological intelligence and marshals the body's resources to heal cuts, mend broken bones, ease breathing, and help with the transition from life to death. Thus, as a healing modality, Reiki fits perfectly into the new paradigm of Alternative Medicine that is emerging in Western health care. This paradigm includes mind and body awareness and prevention techniques. Over the past several years, Reiki's growth among physicians and nurses, psychologist, psychotherapist, ministers, priests, nuns, physical and occupational therapists, and hospice staffs is phenomenal. Some healthcare organizations are endorsing Reiki as part of the ongoing education for their professional staff. These organizations even offer Continuing Education Credit to participants.

Some health care entities feel that Reiki broadens the scope of medical choices and offers an avenue to blend therapies. Since Reiki requires no specific setting or preparation, it easily integrates into all hospital environments. This includes outpatient clinics, emergency rooms, intensive care units, operating rooms, and all other patient settings. It is no problem to implement Reiki into a patient's treatment at any point.

Health providers believe that Reiki is useful alone or as an adjunct treatment. It seamlessly adds to any healthcare professional's medical repertoire. There are many indications for the use of Reiki in the hospital. It helps relieve stress, agitation, and acute or chronic pain. It is helpful as an aid for sleeping and as an energizer. Promoters find that Reiki provides relief for emotions such as grief, anger, or anxiety and provides comfort in palliative care. Another plus that practitioners point out is that there are no side effects or contraindications for Reiki. Reiki is noninvasive and appropriate for all segments of the population.

Reiki is fast becoming a part of *nurse training*, especially in Holistic Nursing and Hospice. The International Center for Reiki Training provides continuing education programs approved by the American Holistic Nurses Association. The Center began in 1988 as the Center for Spiritual Development. It provides spiritual development classes on topics such as past-life regression, although the focus today is exclusively on Reiki training. One technique taught at the Center is a healing *attunement*. It is a process that "opens a spiritual door through which powerful, higher-frequency Reiki energies are able to flow, and through which spirit guides can work more effectively." Articles on the Center's web site include such titles as *"Reiki and Past Lives," "Was Jesus a Reiki Master?" "Reiki and Shamanic Healing," "Reiki as a Spiritual Path," "Organizing a (Reiki) Healing Service in Your Church,"* and *"Knowing Your Reiki Guides."*[47]

Hospice staffs claim that Reiki not only addresses symptoms, but also improves quality of life. A dying person's final weeks of life can be fraught with boredom, frustration, loneliness, depression, and fear. Reiki provides comfort and well-being along with deep relaxation and reduction of pain without sacrificing consciousness. Reiki facilitates the management of severe pain with less medication. Hospice staffs report that Reiki leaves the patient more alert to deal with the emotional issues of closure with family and friends. If the patient is unable to articulate his feelings, Reiki touch provides an avenue of emotional healing at the end of life.

One hospice manager states that as the Universal Life Force flows, it calms and soothes the provider as well as the patient. Anxiety decreases, enabling both the patient and those close to them to focus more on accepting and understanding the impending death, thus facilitating the dual processes of grieving and letting go.

[47] Mooney, Sharon Fish. *Reiki: With Minds Wide Open,* Christian Research Journal, Vol. 29, No. 6 (2006)

SHORTCOMINGS OF REIKI

Although Reiki advocates would have us believe that Reiki is the new "miracle medicine," top medical professionals disagree. According to studies and leading medical opinion, Reiki is not medically effective. The *International Journal of Clinical Practice* reports that, "In total, the trial data for any one condition are scarce and independent replications are not available for each condition. Most trials suffered from methodological flaws such as small sample size, inadequate study design and poor reporting. In conclusion, the evidence is insufficient to suggest that Reiki is an effective treatment for any condition. Therefore the value of Reiki remains unproven".[48]

"The value of Reiki remains unproven".

The Mayo Clinic expresses its opinion about the medical effectiveness of Reiki. Dr. Brent Bauer writes in behalf of the physician's group assigned to explore Reiki's potential in therapeutic use. He states that, "Similar to Healing Touch, the benefits associated with Reiki may come from its ability to help promote relaxation. There is little, if any health risk from the therapy. However, there is also little evidence that it can effectively treat specific conditions. It's up to you if you think it's worth your money to give it a try".[49]

---

[48] *International Journal of Clinical Practice* Volume 62 Issue 6, Pages 947-954. Pub online: 10 (Accessed October 14, 2022).

[49] Bauer, Brent M.D., (2007). *Book of Alternative Medicine.* New York, New York: Time Inc. p. 113.

IS REIKI A MEDICAL THERAPY OR A RELIGION?

Reiki touts itself as a treatment for many diseases and conditions. However, the practice is not medically verifiable and is lacking in scientific evidence. Medical Reiki is emerging as popular school of thought in the healing community today. Some practitioners focus on promoting the medical legitimacy of Reiki in the scientific community. They take part in research projects and lobby for Reiki's use in the hospital and doctors offices. They teach Reiki to healthcare professionals, doctors and nurses. They also lobby insurance companies to cover the cost of Reiki sessions.

As a whole, conventional medicine clearly states that Reiki has little or no medicinal value. Those who peddle it as an alternative therapy to medical care are in grave error. According to the best medical institutions in this country, Reiki is not effective.

As we have seen, Reiki is foremost a religious idea. It is a system of healing born in Japan out of the practices of Buddhism. Reiki's philosophies are spiritual and not medical. Though technically not a religion or even a formal spiritual practice, Reiki has become precisely that for many people. It acts as a foundation for spiritual and magical awareness. Reiki opens the door to a world abounding in Eastern spirituality.[50]

For Christians, it is easy to identify the ties that Reiki has with not only Buddhism and its pantheistic teaching, and also with its connection to a myriad of occult practices. As believers, we must remember that we deal with the reality of Satan's influence every day. Satan is *"like a roaring lion, walking about, seeking whom he may devour"* (1 Peter 5:8). His power is real and exists today. Like the Egyptian magicians who withstood Moses centuries ago, Satan will use his abilities to mimic and decry the power of God whenever and wherever he can. This is what Reiki does – mimics the power of God, offering sick and hurting people an avenue of healing outside of God's provision. We must take a stand against the powers of darkness and refuse to allow them a foothold in our lives or in our health care system.

---

[50]   Penczak, Christopher. (2004). *Magick of Reiki Focused Energy for Healing: Ritual and Spiritual Development.* St. Paul, Minnesota: Llewellyn Publications. pp. 227, 228

STUDY QUESTIONS

SPIRITUAL HEALING THROUGH REIKI

1. What percentage of U. S. Hospitals use Reiki?

2. What does the word Reiki mean?

3. What are attunements?

4. Recount in your own words how Dr. Usui developed Reiki.

5. What are the four Reiki Symbols and how is each used?

6. What is the purpose of the Reiki Symbols? When are they given?
    How are they used?

7. What is the purpose of the Three Degrees of Initiation?

8. What are the central beliefs of the practice of Reiki?

9. What are some of the occult practices used in Reiki?

10. Why is Reiki an attractive practice to medical communities?

11. How are Reiki's claims to being an effective treatment being countered by medical institutions?

12. What is the religious basis of Reiki? How does it conflict with Christianity?

CHAPTER 7
THE "SCIENCE" OF THERAPEUTIC TOUCH

CHAPTER 7
THE "SCIENCE" OF THERAPEUTIC TOUCH

"For me, the safest place is out on a limb."

— Shirley MacLaine

Therapeutic Touch has its roots in the occult practices of Oscar Estabany. A retired military Colonel, Oscar Estabany became world-renowned for his power to heal both people and animals with his hands. Estabany, or Mr. E. as he was later called, became aware of this gift when he was in the cavalry and his horse fell ill. He spent the night massaging the animal and by daylight, the horse recovered.

Scientists at McGill University studied Mr. E.'s method. In their double-blind trials, these scientists found that Estabany decreased the healing time for wounded mice by 22%. Two nurses, Dolores Krieger PhD, Prof. Emeritus of nursing at New York University, and Dora Kunz, a clairvoyant and healer, spent much time observing Mr. E and were amazed at his results. Based on their studies of Mr. Estabany and other healers, Krieger and Kunz founded the healing method known as Therapeutic Touch.

They developed this new technique in the early 1970s. Kunz, then the president of the American Theosophical Society, and Krieger, were part of a group observing a series of sessions conducted by Oscar Estabany. During these sessions, he used laying on of hands to treat people for a wide variety of ailments.

Kunz, a clairvoyant since birth, watched him, using her extraordinary powers of sensing. Krieger used medical tools and strategies to measure and record blood pressure, pulse, and any other visible signs of change in the people treated. Outcomes of Estabany's sessions were impressive, and Kunz felt she understood the process well enough to teach it. In turn, she taught it to Krieger who had moderate success right from the start.

Krieger dreamed of nurses offering this healing method to patients. Together, Krieger and Kunz began to do just that. Krieger offered the first Therapeutic Touch course for graduate nurses at New York University under the title, *"Frontiers of Nursing"* in 1979. It was remarkably popular and continues to be a part of the curriculum in 80 medical schools. Over 80,000 nurses have been trained in Therapeutic Touch.[51] Because it is part of the nursing community, Therapeutic Touch appeals to the nursing profession. Therefore, Therapeutic Touch is widely taught to healthcare professionals, and nurses in particular. In fact, the therapy is part of many basic nursing textbooks.

Kunz and Krieger, define Therapeutic Touch as a balanced, even flow of vital energy within a person and their environment. This idea firmly connects Therapeutic Touch to Hindu philosophy and uses it as a conceptual framework. Krieger speculated that *"prana"* or the *"vital energy"* in Hinduism was the medium transferred during the Therapeutic Touch process.

> *"Therapeutic Touch is a form of healing that uses the practice called 'laying on of hands.'"*

The Therapeutic Touch website continues developing a definition of Therapeutic Touch stating that, Therapeutic Touch is a form of healing that uses the practice called "laying on of hands" to correct or balance energy fields. The word "touch" is misleading because there is no direct physical touch involved. Instead, the hands move just over the body. Therapeutic Touch theorizes that the body, mind, and emotions form a complex energy field. According to Therapeutic Touch, health is an indication of a balanced energy field, and illness represents imbalance. They suggest that Therapeutic Touch can help to heal wounds, reduce pain, and promote relaxation.

The power from which Therapeutic Touch operates is the *"Vital Life Energy"* or *"energy field"*. Although scientists differ on the nature and relevance of the energy field, the idea of this field is part of many religious

---

[51]   Shannon, Scott. (2001). *Handbook of Complementary and Alternative Therapies in Mental Health.* San Diego, CA: Academic Press. p. 231,232.

systems. In the ancient medical techniques of India and China, it is part of the *Universal Life Energy*, an idea familiar to both Buddhism and Hinduism. Religious leaders claim that this energy exists throughout the body and is responsible for maintaining normal physiological, psychological, and spiritual functions. In Traditional Chinese Medicine, this energy is called *qi* (pronounced "chee") while in India's *Ayurvedic* medicine it is called *prana*.

OVERVIEW OF HOW THERAPEUTIC TOUCH WORKS

Scientists are not certain how Therapeutic Touch works. There are few studies, and scientific investigators have so far not detected the energy field advocated by Therapeutic Touch practitioners. Still, two theories are under consideration to explain how it works.

One theory is the pain associated with a physically or emotionally painful experience (such as infection, injury, or a difficult relationship) remains in the body's cells. The pain stored in the cells is disrupted, and prevents some cells from working properly with others. This results in disease. Practitioners of Therapeutic Touch believe the therapy restores health by re-establishing communication between cells.

The other theory operates from the principles of quantum physics. Blood, which contains iron, circulates in our bodies and forms an electromagnetic field. According to this theory, at one time we could all easily see this field (called an *aura*), but now only certain individuals, such as those who practice Therapeutic Touch, have this ability.

Therapeutic Touch flows from the idea that optimal health requires a balanced flow of life energy. Practitioners, state that they sense negative energy through their hands and then send healthy energy back to clients. When receiving Therapeutic Touch, clients usually feel warmth, relaxation, and pain relief. The practitioner describes the energy as hot or cold, active or passive, blocked or free. There are seven regions (the chakras) of the body where energy exists – the head, throat, heart, stomach, lower abdomen, sacral region, knees, and feet. The practitioner merely allows the body's own healing mechanisms to operate. The role of the practitioner is simply to facilitate this process.

STAGES OF THE THERAPEUTIC SESSION

Therapeutic Touch sessions occur in the following stages with small variations from therapist to therapist.

Centering: at the beginning of the session, the therapist engages in a few moments of quiet meditation or deep breathing. Centering helps practitioners connect with this energy and become attuned with the energy field of the client.

Assessment: the therapist stands or kneels in front of the receiver as she rapidly passes her hands several inches away from the body. A healthy person's field will feel whole and unbroken. In an unhealthy person, the therapist may feel hot or cold spots, a tingling feeling, or even just an intuitive sense there is an imbalance.

Unruffling: the goal of the session is to release blocked energy and enable it to flow freely throughout the body. The therapist moves her hands down the receiver's body in rhythmic, sweeping motions. At the end of each stroke, she shakes the energy off her fingers, like shaking off water.

Transferring Energy: the practitioner fills areas of the body where she senses an energy deficit in the client. She does not give away her own energy, rather, she is a conduit for the universal life energy and directs it to the receiver. She positions her hands on weak spots, directing energy to flow there.

BIOGRAPHY OF DORA KUNZ

Dora Kunz used her clairvoyant abilities in numerous medical contexts for many decades. She worked with physicians in paranormal diagnosis and in counseling patients. Kunz states that she is the 14th generation in her family able to promote healing based on reading people's auras. Neurologist Schafica Karagulla has recorded some of her work with Kunz on epilepsy and other disorders in her book, *Breakthrough to Creativity* (DeVorss, 1986). As stated earlier, Mrs. Kunz and Delores Krieger developed Therapeutic Touch as an application of various healing techniques. Since the early 1970s, Kunz and Krieger have held annual healer's workshops for health professionals. Kunz also lectures and gives workshops on meditation and healing. President of the Theosophical Society in America since 1975, she is the chairperson of its publishing house and editor in chief of its journal, *The American Theosophist.*[52]

QUANTUM PHYSICS OR SPIRITUALITY

Dora Kunz explains the operating mechanism of Therapeutic Touch in two ways: the concept of Eastern religion and Quantum Physics. The first is a spiritual explanation, the second a reductionistic scientific model. Together, the two seem mutually incongruent. One may ask, "What does a religious idea have to do with science?" From Mrs. Kunz's standpoint, they are intrically and dynamically related. This mixture of the spiritual and scientific ingredients can make her theorizing confusing to follow.

Kunz's first hypothesis is that the basic physical energy or vitality comes from *prana,* central to Hindu philosophy. *Prana* enters the body through an enigmatic mechanism known as a chakra that she describes as an energy "transformer".

Second, Kunz explains Therapeutic Touch's efficacy by using an element of quantum physics called field theory. Field Theory is a concept first introduced by Albert Einstein to explain the operative state of energy. Kunz distorts Einstein's theory to introduce the idea that "Every individual living organism can be described both as a physical entity and as a system of energy fields that are constantly interacting with the environment. This field, like all known to science permeates space. Each individual is a localization of energy within these universal fields. The fields, which constitutes a person include:

1. The vital field and is associated with the etheric body.

2. The emotional field often called the aura.

3. The mental field referred to as the embodiment of our thinking as well as our concepts and ideas.

4. The intuitional field, which is characterized by creativity and compassion, and is a source of healing.

---

[52]   Kunz, Dora. (1985). *Spiritual Healing.* Wheaton, IL: Quest Books: The Theosophical Publishing House. p. xiii.

As mentioned previously, these four fields are external to the physical body and have distinctive features. There are variations in the human fields, just as red, blue, and yellow are parts of the spectrum of white light. These fields continuously interact with one another through the chakras and they affect the fields of others. According to Kunz, this interpersonal interaction keeps us alive.

Kunz believes that to maintain a state of health, the energy in all the fields must be incoming, outgoing, and free flowing. A pathological state takes over when the energy blocks or constricts any of the fields, causing the flow to falter or slow down. As the fields receive energy from the vital life force, practitioners need to learn how to replenish it.[53]

THERAPEUTIC TOUCH AND SPIRITUALITY

Although Kunz tries to gain credibility for Therapeutic Touch by using scientific jargon, we will see the primary activating mechanism behind Therapeutic Touch is in the spiritual dimension. She writes, "I have long felt the absence of God from our hospitals. I often notice the absence of signs of spirituality in hospitals not run by religious orders. One of my associates, Richard Selzer, a surgeon and writer, shares my feeling eloquently in his short story *Absence of Windows*. He states, "I fear that having bricked up our windows, we have lost more than the breeze; we have severed a celestial connection. How do we re-establish this connection? Obviously, we cannot bring the windows back, but must create a new healing environment".[54]

"I have long felt the absence of God from our hospitals".

Kunz's Theosophical tendencies appear in the way in which she merges spiritualities in support of her theory. An example of this is in her book, *Spiritual Healing*, where she writes, "I feel also that I should touch on the work that has been done by the spiritualistic mediums in giving advice. This advice, when followed, brings complete restoration of health or

---

[53]   Ibid. pp. 220-223.
[54]   Ibid. p. 127.

improvement. In addition, everyone has heard about the amazing cures of hopeless diseases at the shrine at Lourdes".[55]

Kunz illustrates this tendency to merge religious ideas even further when she quotes from an evangelist, the Bible and a Chinese philosopher in the space of two paragraphs. She writes that, "at present the drug addiction among the young is a matter of great concern. Recently I heard a speaker comment on the fact that those healers who brought a religious element to bear seems to get a more substantial result. Twice on the radio in the last few months, I have heard of the work of the Teen Challenge movement. In order to understand how Teen Challenge came about, I heartily recommend reading its amazing book *The Cross and the Switchblade*, by David Wilkerson, its founder.

This reminds me of the New Testament saying, 'the Father knows what you have need of before you ask'. It also reminds us of the advice of the Chinese philosopher 'to open our eyes to the wonder of living'. The restoration to complete physical wholeness is something that we ardently and earnestly work for, regardless of the particular discipline that we follow".[56] From these syncretistic statements, one can easily connect Kunz's theosophical worldview with her work in Therapeutic Touch. Obviously, one of Kunz's primary beliefs is there *are many pathways to healing, and all are equally valid.*

Another illustration of her blending of religious ideas includes a quote from sources found in Spiritism, Christianity and Buddhism. "There are individuals who have the gift of revitalizing exhausted etheric bodies. Others do not have this gift, but have higher abilities to heal. Still others by clairvoyant insight can make more accurate diagnoses than our coarse physical methods can achieve. In the book *At the Feet of the Master*, we hear that we are to, 'Use our thought power every day for good purposes. Think each day of someone whom you know to be in sorrow or suffering or in need of help, and pour out loving thoughts upon him. Learn to distinguish *the God in everyone*. You can help your brother through that which you have in common with him -- and *that is the divine life*. Learn how to arouse that Life in him, learn how to appeal to that in him, so you shall save your brother from wrong'".[57] Kunz's spirituality is muddled and confused. Certainly none of these traditions would approve of meshing

---

[55] Ibid. p. 65

[56] Ibid. 63-65.

[57] Ibid. 66, 67.

their ideas together. Kunz attempts to join religious ideas and systems that are diametrically opposed to one another to support her theory and mold them into an alternative therapy that she has christened Therapeutic Touch.

THE PRACTICE OF SPIRITISM AND THERAPEUTIC TOUCH

Notice that Kunz not only incorporates Eastern religion as part of Therapeutic Touch, she also incorporates Spiritism and occult beliefs to endorse her ideas. In a record of her own personal journey into the occult, Dora Kunz writes, "Elizabeth Kubler-Ross encouraged me to attend a workshop with Carl and Stephanie Simonton. They told me that during an exercise in guided imagery I would meet an inner guide. The mechanic within me said, 'This is all ridiculous.' Yet in the meditation, along came George. *George is a spiritual figure who guides me.* Since then I have met other guides often seen by mediums. I only see guides in imaginary exercises and sense them around me. However, mediums have seen them standing around me at my lectures or workshops. A new world opened up for a mechanic that could exist no longer without a belief system".[58]

Kunz also promotes mediumship as a method for contacting the spirits of the dead. She remembers one patient of hers, a physician, who was naturally scientific and found it all hard to believe. She states that she asked him one day when he was ill in the hospital, if he was ready to die. His response was that "considering the alternative, no."

Three months after his death, a student came to interview her and gave her a card containing a message. The student said she had been at a healing circle and told everyone she was going to interview me the following day. The medium present asked if there was a message from Dr. Siegel. She wrote out the message she received on a card. The card said, to 'Bernie from Frank, love and peace. If I had known the journey was so easy, I would have bought the package a long time ago. I wouldn't have resisted so much.' The language on the card was Frank's way of referring to my teachings. He never bought the package".[59]

---

58   Ibid. pp. 48-51.
59   Ibid. p.123.

"The truth is that Therapeutic Touch is not an alternative form of medicine; it is a spiritual practice and does not belong in hospital environments".

Dora Kunz attempted to validate Therapeutic Touch as a medical modality based on the science of quantum physics and field theory. In this, she was not as effective, as her co-founder, Delores Krieger, who used her science background much more effectively. The truth for Kunz is that the activating agency behind Therapeutic Touch is not science, but spirituality. Kunz roots her spirituality in her own Theosophical beliefs. The theory behind Therapeutic Touch integrates a spiritual mix that blends Eastern religious ideas, Christianity and Spiritism to formulate the basis of her thinking. The most frightening aspect of Therapeutic Touch is how it is being so widely used in medical training. The truth is that Therapeutic Touch is not an alternative form of medicine; it is a spiritual practice and does not belong in hospital environments.

DELORES KRIEGER CO-FOUNDER OF THERAPEUTIC TOUCH

Delores Krieger, R.N., PhD is professor emeritus at New York University. In 1972, she and Dora Kunz founded Therapeutic Touch as an alternative healing therapy. Krieger states that tests prove its reliability and validity with extensive research. Eventually, many health care institutions adopted it as an extension of their professional practice.

By the end of the 20th century, 100 medical centers and health agencies were including the practice of Therapeutic Touch in there inpatient and outpatient services. The master's level course that Krieger created in 1975 for New York University, marks the first time that a medically uncertified program became part of an accredited college or university's curriculum. At the university's suggestion, *"Frontiers and Nursing"* became part of their conspectus of courses. NYU continues teaching this course, and its curriculum has become a model for graduate classes in colleges and universities in many countries throughout the world.

Presently, Therapeutic Touch is taught in more than 80 foreign countries. A list of 70 medical schools in North America and about 75 medical centers teaching Therapeutic Touch is in the appendix of Krieger's books.

FIELD THEORY

While Dora Kunz tried to rationalize and attribute scientific validity to Therapeutic Touch, she did not have the scientific or medical knowledge to do so. On the other hand, Delores Krieger is clinically trained and much more adept at providing a scientific basis for Therapeutic Touch. Krieger's entire approach to Therapeutic Touch relies on quantum physics and field theory. The difference is that she moved beyond the time-space concept of field theory and taught the existence of other fields as well. She also applied her speculation about field theory to the realm of psychology. Krieger was among the first to conceptualize the existence of a "behavioral field". She further extended her thinking into the area of faith postulating the existence of a "spiritual field". Clear-minded thinkers are among the first to recognize that it is simply wrong headed to apply the objective science of quantum physics to the subjective studies of behavior and spirituality; they just do not mesh.

In her seminal work on Therapeutic Touch, Krieger explains the effects of field theory as the operational force that makes it work. She explains that as "the post-industrial era blossomed in the work of Einstein and others, it was obvious the theoretical framework of physics held a new and prominent place among rest of the sciences. Chemistry, medicine and biology, closely followed by psychology and the social sciences, adopted these ideas as originally conceived in physics. Further developmental thinking encouraged other sciences to utilize them as ingredients in their own studies as well".

The development of the Universal Healing Field in Therapeutic Touch is analogous to the ideas incorporated during the same era in other psychosocial disciplines. Krieger said that Therapeutic Touch deals with experiences that transcend the personality and the place of the therapist and creates a different state of interiority. However, these states of consciousness are difficult to describe by the physical sciences.

Krieger believes that the idea of a Universal Healing Field involves a tacit understanding that there is a non-physical dimension of time and space. The field where healing takes place, is universal because all living beings have the innate capacity to heal themselves. She states that they also have the natural potential to help others in need. In this sense, the Universal Healing Field is the source of all healing.[60]

THE VITAL ENERGY FIELD

Like Kunz, Krieger did not limit herself to the realm of science to explain the healing method she calls Therapeutic Touch. She moved from the sciences into the area of the metaphysical and spiritual. Similar to Reiki, she contends there is a *Vital Energy Field* that when directed to those who are ill, conveys healing. However, Krieger distances herself from scientific and objective explanations, and attributes this energy field to Eastern philosophies based in experience.

She argues for the existence of a chasm between the philosophical and spiritual elements that separate Western and Eastern perceptions of thought. Krieger asserts that in the West, the basis of scientific inquiry is logic and objectivity. She believes that inquiry in other cultures is experiential and seems illogical, at least as far as basic assumptions are concerned. It is this experiential knowledge that has come to us from developing countries, which much of our understanding of human vital energies has arisen. As noted, estimates find that there are at least 97 cultures in the world, which recognize that an energy field surrounds each individual.

"It is often difficult for Westerners to accept that other cultures and sophisticated knowledge existed before the era of Christianity".

Continuing her treatise on the existence of the Vital Life Energy and its dynamic interaction with the human energy field, Krieger steps even further away from conventional medicine and deeper into the area of Eastern mysticism. She admits that most of her work builds on a Hindu

---

[60] Krieger, Delores. (2002). *Therapeutic Touch As Transpersonal Healing.* New York: Lantern Books. pp.32-36

paradigm. She says that, "It is often difficult for Westerners to accept that other cultures and sophisticated knowledge existed before the era of Christianity. Nevertheless, it is a historical fact that the histories of both India and China go back approximately 5,000 years in their studies of healing. Both of these ancient cultures hold that the ultimate cause of illness is depletion, congestion, or imbalance of the rhythmic *vital energy* flow. This energy is called *prana* in Indian literature and *qi* in Chinese. Of the two, the logic and assumptions of the Indian form are more accessible to the Western mind. So it is the Indian framework of reference about *subtle energies* that has been used as a model during the development of Therapeutic Touch".[61]

LEVELS OF CONSCIOUSNESS

Krieger addresses another metaphysical concept postulating the existence of different levels of consciousness. Psychologists support the existence of two forms of consciousness: the conscious mind and the subconscious mind. Krieger wants to extend these even further, hypothesizing the existence of multiple forms of consciousness. She uses this idea to support the spiritual and metaphysical concepts she incorporates into Therapeutic Touch. During the development of this part of her theory, she attempts to use the objective and scientific to validate the non-scientific and subjective aspects of her work.

First, she discusses the *chakras as a level of consciousness*. She states, "Western tradition treats the physical body as the basic human manifestation. The writings of Eastern schools of thought agree that the beginnings of human consciousness and its embodiment in physical matter occurs at the transpersonal rather than at the physical level". In a manner said to be dependent on the individual's *karma*, she accepts the idea of reincarnation as fact. According to Krieger, a force generated by one's actions in previous lifetimes determines the nature of one's current life and orchestrates growth and development.

Second, she hypothesizes the existence of what she calls the *Unitary Consciousness*. She continues saying that this form of consciousness includes the innate ability of the mind to tap into the paranormal. Krieger asserts

---

[61] Ibid. pp. 42-44.

that intensive studies on extended human abilities, also known as ESP, accepts that human consciousness transcends the limits of the functions of the brain. She states that she can corroborate transcultural teachings on meditation, visualization, and imagery.

Third, Krieger stresses that another form of consciousness exists pertaining to consciousness outside of the self. She calls this the "transpersonal consciousness". She agrees with Groff's extensive studies of the human psyche. Krieger concludes that using psychedelic drugs to alter states of consciousness is a brilliant idea. She states that this came on the heels of the introduction of Indian, Tibetan, and Chinese philosophies into the United States.

The range of reported experiences based on drug experimentation is all but inconceivable. There are detailed accounts of ancestral experiences, racial and collective memories, historical events, and an entire spectrum of extra sensory experiences that she sees as valid transpersonal events. Krieger assert that transpersonal experiences have many strange characteristics that shatter the most fundamental assumptions of the materialistic and mechanistic worldview.[62]

The working basis for Krieger's theory of Therapeutic Touch is complex. She begins with objective science laying a framework for Therapeutic Touch, and then introduces the bizarre concept of the *human field theory*, the *vital energy force* and multiple *levels of consciousness*.

All along, she slowly begins a slippery descent into the realm of Eastern religion and finally into the abyss of the occult itself. This occurs as she expands from theory to theory. Her expansion on field theory opens up the possibility of *other realms of existence*. Her acceptance of the value of Eastern subjectivity over the West's focus on empiricism *opens up avenues to the metaphysical*. While her psychological presuppositions regarding different levels of consciousness *opens the door to the dark realities of the occult*.

THE SPIRITUALITY OF THERAPEUTIC TOUCH

As shown previously, the spirituality of Therapeutic Touch is primarily Indian Hinduism. It is equally important to clarify that Therapeutic Touch is not only a stream of Eastern religious thought, but is also connected to the occult.

---

[62]   Ibid. pp. 119,120.

Delores Krieger emphasizes a link between the therapist and client that she refers to as mind-to-mind communication. Its takes little imagination to realize that she is talking about *telepathy* as part of her healing technique. She states that "inter-mind" connections occur easily between healer and healee. According to Krieger, this telepathic bond frequently remains strong between Therapeutic Touch therapists and their clients for some time.

Another form of occult practice used by Krieger is *channeling* or *mediumship*. As the therapist reaches out to the client, while centering the inner self, the client becomes aware of a different level of consciousness. To clients, this sense of consciousness may reflect an awareness of *otherworldly beings*. It is at this time that an *inner source of unusual helpers and allies* slip through from another reality to help us or to heal us.

Krieger relates, "As you hear your own voice relating these impressions and know them to be true, it is almost as if one is standing beside herself. With something akin to awe, one hears as if from some source other than oneself, a well-developed synthesis of information and an evaluation of the healee's condition".[63]

Ms. Krieger has also appropriates the psychic gift of *Clairaudience* -- the ability to hear the supernatural. She delves into the practice of animism as well. To her, it does not seem too strange to hear that many who undergo changes in awareness feel that they can also communicate with and understand other sentient beings, such as trees, birds, and animals.

Krieger lists a litany of occult practices that she uses openly, and in no uncertain terms. She mentions several Spiritist techniques that come to mind as a means of healing. These include *mind-to-mind communication* with other persons without regard to geographical separation; *psychokinesis*, the ability to move objects without physically touching them; *clairvoyance* and *clairaudience*, the ability to see and hear beyond the usual range of human perception; *precognition*, knowing in the present, details about future events. She adds several other exotic states of consciousness to this list as well. Of course, we must not forget the primary occult practice used by Krieger and her therapists – *Clairsentience* or the ability to perceive the supernatural through touch!

---

[63]   Krieger, Delores. (1987). *Living the Therapeutic Touch: Healing as a Lifestyle.* Dodd, Mead & Company: New York, New York. p. 76.

THE STORY OF MY FRIENDS THE TREES

The following is a firsthand account Krieger uses to highlight her own increasing sensitivity to the paranormal through Therapeutic Touch. Ultimately, she believes that all practitioners can develop the same sensitivity. It is worth noticing that her method of communication is with inanimate objects. This is a form of the American Indian and African practice called *Animism*. Please follow along as she writes.

"I can talk about trees, and the consciousness that unfolds from them, from personal experience. A personal incident that is still very vivid in my own mind has served to heighten the sensitivity of Therapeutic Touch therapists. A friend of mine had flown with a young Irish Setter dog directly from Paris, France to Pumpkin Hollow in New England. This is where Dora and I had done the original research and development of Therapeutic Touch. During the night, the dog left, and did not return. In the morning, the 50 or so people at the Hollow formed search parties and drove off in their cars to find her dog. I did not own a car at that time, and so I set off with my own dog to search the meadows and back woods.

> *"I can talk about trees, and the consciousness that unfolds from them, from personal experience."*

It was a very hot summer day and after an hour or so of search, I sought out the cool shade of a large and very old maple tree. I sat with my back against its trunk and idly watched my dog sniffing out the territory. I thought of trying to get in touch with the maple tree. In a few minutes, I centered myself with what I thought was the appropriate chakra to communicate with this tree. I visualized the lost dog as clearly as I could and asked the tree if he knew where I could find her. I was aware of a response within myself and almost immediately, in lucid terms, he told me to go toward a well-known lake and to ask people as I went. Somehow, the message instilled a sense of urgency in me. I quickly whistled up my dog and took off in the direction of the lake without questioning the instructions.

I cut across the meadow with a sense of purpose until I got to the lake road. I then stopped at every farmhouse on the way to find out whether anyone had seen the dog, since this was my interpretation of the instruction from the tree. Nevertheless, I arrived at the lake without having turned up a clue as to the whereabouts of the dog.

By now, it was late in the afternoon, and as I looked at my tired pooch, I thought we had been following a will-o'-the-wisp that had originated as a figment of my own imagination. There was a freestanding telephone booth at the lakeshore. I phoned a friend at the Hollow and asked her to drive over to the lake and pick us up. It was about then that the miracle happened. As I looked up from the phone, I saw a middle-aged couple, evidently tourists, walking along the lake's shoreline. Remembering the tree's advice to ask people as I walked to the lake, I went forward with some ambivalence. When I agreed to meet them and ask them about the lost dog, it seemed incredulous. The wife turned to her husband and asked, 'Dear, wasn't that the Red Setter that was with the gatekeeper when we drove back to the hotel last night'? The husband agreed, and we all walked over the nearby isthmus of land to a hotel situated on a bit of the isle in the lake.

The husband sought out the hotel manager, who brought us to the gate. 'Yes', he said. The dog we described had come to the gatehouse around 11 PM, looking as if she had been running. He had given the dog some cool milk, but regretted that hotel policy would not allow him to keep the dog. Around midnight one of the chambermaids came back to the hotel with her brother-in-law. The brother-in-law noticed the dog and offered to give her a good home. The gatekeeper gave the dog to the brother-in-law, who drove off with her.

That was all the gateman could tell us, but he did look for the chamber maid at our request. She confirmed the story and told us that the dog was now in a very large town about 50 miles from where we were. She gave me her brother-in-law's address and phone number. Thanks to the explicit advice from the old maple tree, dog and mistress were soon reunited".

Krieger concludes her story saying, "Today, the stigma has been removed from talking with one's plants. It will not seem too extraordinary to learn that many who undergo these changes in awareness feel that they can also communicate with and understand other sentient beings such as trees, birds, and animals as well. They will realize that they can communicate with them just as they do with other human beings. Of course, these are the people who have a green thumb and that the creatures seek out".[64]

---

[64]   Krieger, Delores. (2002). *Therapeutic Touch As Transpersonal Healing*. New York: Lantern Books. pp. 164-168.

A HEALING MODALITY OR A SPIRITUAL PRACTICE

What is the medical consensus regarding the effectiveness of Therapeutic Touch as an integrative alternative therapy? Two of the most prodigious names in the medical field have studied its effectiveness and announced their findings.

The Mayo Clinic in Rochester, Minnesota reports, "Therapeutic Touch resembles the religious concept of 'laying on of hands', where healing power flow from the minister's hands to a patient. However, Therapeutic Touch is not a part of a religious concept. Practitioners believe that by transferring healing energy through their hands to the body, they can reduce pain, stress and anxiety. Many conventional health care providers are skeptical of Therapeutic Touch, which is unsupported by solid research.

More research is necessary to determine if Therapeutic Touch has *any* health benefits. The scientific evidence about this controversial technique is lacking. Thus, many conventional health care providers feel this technique has little or no benefit".[65]

> *"More research is necessary to determine if Therapeutic Touch has any health benefits".*

In a 1998 study that appeared in the *Journal of the American Medical Association* reported on the efficacy of Therapeutic Touch. The evidence against its value was conclusive, leaving no room for doubt. According to JAMA, they found no value in the practice of Therapeutic Touch. The results of the study are below:

Context — Therapeutic Touch (TT) is a widely used nursing practice rooted in mysticism but alleged to have a scientific basis. Practitioners of TT claim to treat many medical conditions by using their hands to manipulate a "human energy field" perceptible above the patient's skin.

Objective — To investigate whether TT practitioners can actually perceive a "human energy field."

Design — Twenty-one practitioners with TT experience from 1 to 27 years were tested under blinded conditions to determine whether they could correctly identify which of their hands was closest to the investigator's

[65]   Bauer, Brent M. D. (2002). *Alternative Medicine and Your Health*. Rochester, MN: Mayo Clinic Health Information. pp.21,22

hand. Placement of the investigator's hand was determined by flipping a coin. Fourteen practitioners were tested 10 times each, and 7 practitioners were tested 20 times each.

Main Outcome Measure — Practitioners of TT were asked to state whether the investigator's unseen hand hovered above their right hand or their left hand. To show the validity of TT theory, the practitioners should have been able to locate the investigator's hand 100% of the time. A mean score of score of 50% indicates it is only as effective as chance alone.

Results — Practitioners of TT identified the correct hand in only 123 (44%) of 280 trials, which is close to what would be expected for random chance. There was no significant correlation between the practitioner's score and length of experience. The statistical power of this experiment was sufficient to conclude that if TT practitioners could reliably detect a human energy field, the study would have demonstrated this.

Conclusions — Twenty-one experienced TT practitioners were unable to detect the investigator's "energy field." Their failure to substantiate TT's most fundamental claim is unrefuted evidence that the claims of TT are groundless and that further professional use is unjustified.[66]

CONCLUSIONS REGARDING THERAPEUTIC TOUCH

The question that Therapeutic Touch must answer is it a medical modality that is effective in treating patients? The answer is a resounding no. According to the Mayo Clinic and the *Journal of the American Medical Association,* independent studies found it inefficacious.

Co-founders, Dora Kunz and Delores Krieger, have attempted to shroud their therapy in the trappings of conventional medicine. However, there is nothing conventional about Therapeutic Touch. They explain that its basis is in the sciences of quantum physics, field theory and psychology. Research indicates that this is not true, and that the therapy is congruent with the religious practice of Theosophy, Hinduism and the occult. Therapeutic Touch has more to do with metaphysics and religion than it does with medicine. When compared with traditional healing modalities,

---

[66] A Close Look at Therapeutic Touch. Linda Rosa, BSN, RN; Emily Rosa; Larry Sarner; Stephen Barrett, MD JAMA. 1998;279:1005-1010. (Accessed October 14, 2022).

respected medical institutions conclude that Therapeutic Touch has no medical benefit. To call it a healing modality is a misnomer in terms.

For Christians, we must recognize Therapeutic Touch for what it is – a therapy that is antithetic to faith in Jesus Christ. It has been compared to the gift of "laying on of hands", but it is a practice devoid of the presence and power of the Holy Spirit. It attempts to make itself palatable to Western Christianity, but is in fact a syncretistic practice that meshes the world's religions into one glorious soup. It offers a source of healing outside of the atonement of Jesus Christ and offers in its place a *"doctrine of demons"* (1Timothy 4:1). Its entire technique reeks of spiritual death. Through *Centering*, the therapist *channels* the spirit world. Through *Assessment*, she practices *clairvoyance* and c*lairaudience*. Through *Intervention*, she practices *clairsentience*. God's appraisal of such practices is found in Romans 1:32 which declares, *"Who knowing the judgment of God, that they which commit such things are worthy of death, not only do the same, but have pleasure in them that do them"*.

Christians must avoid any alternative therapy that is opposed to the Gospel of our Lord Jesus Christ. If treatment is one of our options, we should flatly refuse. For Christians working in the medical profession, we must recognize what Therapeutic Touch is and avoid being trained or induced into using it in any way. Therapeutic Touch is not a healing modality; it is an intrinsic evil. It is attempting to penetrate our medical system, our lives and the lives of our patients and families whom we serve.

STUDY QUESTIONS

THE "SCIENCE" OF THERAPEUTIC TOUCH

1. Who are Dora Kunz and Delores Krieger? What are their unique backgrounds and how did come to develop Therapeutic Touch?

2. What influence does Hinduism have on Therapeutic Touch?

3. What are the stages of the Therapeutic Touch session and how is it practiced?

4. Why do Kunz and Krieger attempt to use science (quantum physics, field theory, energy fields, electromagnetic fields and psychology) as a basis for Therapeutic Touch?

5. How does the practice of "syncretism" evidence itself in the spirituality of Therapeutic Touch? Why is this similar to Theosophy?

6. What examples of the occult do you see practiced in Therapeutic Touch?

7. What occult practices does Delores Krieger incorporate in Therapeutic Touch?

8. What is Animism and what role does it play in the Krieger's story, "My Friend's the Trees"?

9. According to the Mayo Clinic and JAMA, how effective is Therapeutic Touch?

10. Why should Christians not become involved with Therapeutic Touch?

CHAPTER 8
A LIE CALLED HEALING TOUCH

CHAPTER 8
A LIE CALLED HEALING TOUCH

*"... get your facts first, and then you can distort
them as much as you please".*
— Mark Twain

At times, people confuse Healing Touch with Therapeutic Touch but they
are not the same. Each has different roots, different founders and function
differently. Although medical schools teach Therapeutic Touch, it has
no formal requirements to become a practitioner. Healing Touch on the
other hand has a well-defined educational program that ends in licensing
through its international board. Let us examine the alternative practice of
Healing Touch to understand its medical and spiritual connections.

BIOGRAPHY OF JANET MENTGEN

Janet Mentgen, RN, BSN (1938-2005) developed the *Healing Touch
Certificate Program* late in her nursing career. She spent the last 25 years
of her life studying, practicing, and teaching energy therapies. Healing
Touch developed from her study and experience with other healers. She
expanded her influence by offering courses in the nursing continuing
education program at Denver Community College in the 1980's. Her
healing practice helped others understand how to implement energy
techniques as emphasized within the curriculum.

The *American Holistic Nurses' Association (AHNA)* honored Janet as
the holistic nurse of the year by in 1988. This citation was awarded for

her outstanding work in teaching touch therapies and for her impact on individuals and the community. AHNA sought to bring energy therapies into their organization. They created an opportunity to teach Healing Touch in Memphis, Tennessee, and in Gainesville, Florida as a pilot project in 1989. Because of its success, Healing Touch became a certificate program of the AHNA in 1990 with 25 programs offered across the U.S. in that first year. Establishing her Colorado Center for Healing Touch, Mentger's for-profit business, created even more opportunities for Healing Touch classes.

HEALING TOUCH INTERNATIONAL

The AHNA began offering certification for Healing Touch practitioners and instructors in 1993. Because of the growth and diversity of practitioners, *Healing Touch International, Inc.,* grew into a formal organization in 1996. This organization exists to administer the certification program while also providing continuing education, and promoting Healing Touch research and health care integration. The AHNA continued to support Healing Touch by providing endorsement for the Healing Touch Certificate Program.

The mission of Healing Touch International, as the professional membership organization, is to "spread healing and light worldwide through the heart-centered practice and teaching of Healing Touch". This non-profit membership and educational organization:

- Administers the Certification process for Healing Touch Practitioners and Instructors
- Sets international standards of practice and an international code of ethics.
- Supports Healing Touch Practitioners and Instructors as they develop, practice and serve communities worldwide
- Promotes and provides resources in health care integration and research in Healing Touch
- Provides opportunities for promotion of and education about Healing Touch.

Today, there are over 20,000 members of Healing Touch International with over 200 certified instructors and nearly 2,000 Certified Healing Touch Practitioners.

Healing Touch continues to expand worldwide and is taught throughout the United States, Canada, Australia, New Zealand, Finland, Sweden, the Netherlands, Germany, Romania, India, South Africa, Trinidad, Italy, and South America. Over 50,000 individuals have taken Healing Touch classes. Classes are available through independent instructors and businesses, universities, and health care facilities. New sections are continually opening and requests are being received from the international community to continue to offer programs. Healing Touch is in harmony with people from all lifestyles.[67]

STAGES IN THE HEALING TOUCH PROCESS

What would a client encounter in a Healing Touch session? From the outset, it would seem benign but differences from regular medical visits would be easily identifiable. The stages of the process are as follows:

- *Initial interview* - the initial interview provides the framework for energetic interventions and intake.
- *Assessment* - assessment of the energy field is like an interview, only it is done with the hands. Any disruption of the energy flow reflects disharmony and suggests the need for further exploration.
- *Documentation* - documentation of the assessment begins with the initial client contact and continues throughout the entire visit. It mentally makes notes of all sensations, even the ones that may seem very subtle.
- *Intervention* - the practitioner can choose many healing interventions in order to make intelligent choices for the greatest effectiveness.
- *Completion and Grounding* - after completion of the interventions, carefully ground the client. After the client returns to awareness in the present, spend some time with the client to obtain feedback.

As with other alternative therapies, the goal of Healing Touch practitioners is the implementation of their method into the health care system. There are many milieus where it is possible to introduce Therapeutic

---

[67]   What Is Healing Touch? https://www.healingbeyondborders.org/index.php/ what-is-healing-touch (Accessed October 15,2022).

Touch into health care settings. Therapists promote its use saying that Healing Touch allows the patient to receive the best possible care, both physically and emotionally. They see that Therapeutic Touch can easily be used in pre and post surgical care, assisting with terminal illness, geriatric care, obstetrics, and unmitigated pain.

THE SCIENTIFIC BASIS OF HEALING TOUCH

In her endeavor to explain Healing Touch, Janet Mentger was careful to lay a scientific framework to explain how it operates. She introduced the idea that electromagnetic fields are the activating force behind her theory. Mentger suggests that a biomedical and electromagnetic interaction supports the basis of energetic healing.

George De la War hypothesized that the detection of electromagnetic emanations from the *auric* field is possible through radionic instruments. He found that measurements of the electromagnetic field correlate with the strengths or weaknesses of plants and that weakness in animals suggests the presence of disease. De la War believes that the energetic concepts in medicine use electricity to promote healing and reduce pain. In the past two decades, orthopedist Robert Becker has measured direct current systems in the human body to detect health and disease. His most revolutionary work was stimulating the body's tissue to regenerate. For example, he stimulated regeneration of frog's legs, which normally does not occur. By reversing the polarity of the electrical charge, Dr. Becker demonstrated that compound fractures in horses are healed by implanting electrodes in a cast that pulses with electric current across the fracture site. Other specialists use electric currents to reduce tumor size and to clear cancers in difficult places to treat diseases such as lung cancer.

"The roots of Healing Touch have more to do with a shamanic approach to healing".

Like others, Mentger linked the scientific basis for Healing Touch with Eastern philosophy. She theorized that the human chakras, meridians, and bio fields are electrical in nature. She felt that inducing currents of electricity was the mechanism behind many Healing Touch techniques.

As Healing Touch practitioners sweep the recipient's body with their fingers, they pass an electromagnetic field near the depleted points in the meridians. The purpose is to create a more powerful meridian flow, which enables the body to heal.

Mentger believed that the energetic anatomy of the chakras act like a sophisticated electrical and electromagnetic information processing system. She states that chakras act like the software, bio fields store the data, and the meridians act to carry the current and provide electrical power to control the system. The chakras receive input from the unlimited supply of energy found in nature and release excess qi when there is an overload.[68]

In a recent statement from Dr. Alford N. Vassall Jr. MD, contributor to the new book, *Audacious Aging*, (*www.Audacious Aging.com*), he speaks from a similar mix of science and metaphysics when he describes the process. "The roots of Healing Touch have more to do with a shamanic approach to healing. Surprisingly, even ancient Judaism has some shamanic roots. In Hebrew, the notion of "holy" actually carries an otherworldly connotation. Nevertheless, though this origin carries with it some spiritual connotations, the actual basis of how this works has more to do with physics and understanding how physics interacts with biology. The acupuncture points demonstrate the points of decreased galvanic skin resistance. In the nature of physics, the flow of electrons produces a perpendicular magnetic field so there is always a circular magnetic flow. This is actually the basis of how motors work and how hydroelectric power generates. In fact, the panoply of magnetic fields within the body allows electromagnetic connection between areas normally considered unrelated. This is responsible largely because Healing Touch is inexplicable by other typical biological understandings within Western concepts.[69]

Healing Touch proponents purport that the mechanism that empowers Healing Touch is measurable. Dr. Benjamin Puhariah measured an 8 Hz magnetic field emanating from healer's hands. In his observations, increased or decreased frequencies seem detrimental to life. Dr. Robert Beck, a nuclear physicist, found that the brain waves of healers across many groups and cultures exhibit the same brainwave pattern, 7.8 through 8 Hz, when

---

[68]   Ibid.

[69]   Alford N Vassall Jr., MD. Contributing author, "Audacious Aging" (unpublished).

giving treatments. These energy patterns fluctuate with the Earth's normal magnetic field resonance of 7.828 Hz. This pattern is called a Shuman Wave. The healer's brain synchronizes in both frequency and phase with the Shuman Waves. This is part of the theory of field coupling. This coupling appears to provide access to a large field of energy for the work of healing. Comparisons of energetic patterns in the bio field are found across the spectrum of medical diagnosis through practitioner's reports.

Regardless of the scientific explanations that Mentger and others attempt to use to validate Healing Touch, they are not satisfied unless they also add a spiritual explanation as well. Mentger's theory moves away from a purely scientific explanation and drifts into the realm of metaphysics, religion and the occult.

BEYOND SCIENCE

Healing Touch views the nature of healing very differently than the traditional medical model. It differentiates between *curing* and *healing* to advocate for treatments outside of the mainstream.

Practitioners state that in the current Western model of medical care, the goal is symptom removal or cure. *Cure* in the dictionary sense, is something that corrects, heals, or alleviates the harmful disease process. The word *cure* derives from the Latin word *cura*, or care *of the soul*. There is little in current mainstream healthcare that addresses healing or care of the soul. If the goal of health is merely to be symptom free, by giving drugs to remove pain, or surgery to remove the cancer tumor, that is all that is required. Curing then, in current usage of the term, is quite different philosophically from healing.

The philosophy inherent to Healing Touch departs further from the scientific model of medicine touching on psychogenic and metaphysical concepts. It presupposes that intrinsic in the concept of healing is a wider interpretation of our human reality. Mentger believed that illness is not only a physical problem but indicates an imbalance with other aspects of one's life as well. True well-being is much more than homeostasis in the organs. It is a harmonious evolution within physical, emotional, mental, and spiritual aspects of our being.

Mentger borrows ideas about healing from Eastern philosophical viewpoints as well. It is not difficult to see that her ideas of Healing Touch derive from Hindu, Buddhist and even African traditions that go back thousands of years. Many elements of her practice also include the occult.

In her book, *Healing Touch: a Guide for Practitioners,* her long time associate Dorethea Hover-Kramer, explains these concepts in even more detail. She writes that, "in some ancient African beliefs, sickness or injury was understood as a process in which the individual was out of *alignment with the animal spirits*, ancestral dead, or deities. In the Orient, ancient practices work with the flow of *the sacred energy*, called *Qi*. *T'ai Qi* and *Qi Gong* are two practices known in the West that help to improve *the vital life force* to maintain health.

Acupuncture, an increasingly well-known health promoting modality, stimulates the movement of Qi along energy pathways, known as meridians. Another Eastern practice, known for 5000 years, is the *Ayurvedic* tradition contained within Yoga. In this tradition, activation of the human energy forces is used to balance individual's basic constitution for self-healing and maintaining of balance".[70]

HEALING TOUCH AND THE OCCULT

Not only does Healing Touch incorporate Eastern religious ideas and philosophies into its practice, it also delves into the realm of the occult. We can illustrate this in the following ways.

Practitioners incorporate the reading of *auras.* The aura is an etheric body outside of the physical body that is observable by clairvoyants. It consists of four layers: 1). the vital layer, associated with the physical body; 2). the emotional layer, which extends just beyond this; 3). the mental layer, which embodies our thinking and emotions and: 4). the intuitive layer, sometimes called the astral body which relates to the spiritual dimension.

"The transpersonal state is an opening to the Universe to connect with spirits and angels allowing the flow of energy through the therapist".

---

[70]   Hover-Kramer, Dorethea. 2002. *Healing Touch: A Guidebook for Practitioners.* Albany, New York: Delmar: Thompson Learning. pp. 12-14.

Therapists practice *Centering* in which they enter a *transpersonal state*, *channeling* the vital force energy. The transpersonal state is an opening to the Universe to connect with *spirits* and *angels* allowing the flow of energy through the therapist. In essence, this is a form of mediumship. In this state, therapists use *clairvoyance* and *clairaudience* to see and hear religious figures like Buddha, Jesus and Mary, or deceased family members who provide them with information and guidance in the healing process. Most important is the use of *clairsentience,* or touch to allow healing energy to channel into the client's chakra system to produce healing.

Mentger proposed that the therapist could develop *Higher Perceptual Senses*. She postulates that, there is a need for the healers to align themselves with a "*Higher Power*" in order to sense the unlimited supply of energy within nature. In this process, the therapist becomes a conduit for the Universal Life Energy, the Source, or Higher Power. The development of higher perceptual senses is necessary to facilitate healing. During the Healing Touch session, the therapist clears herself of her thoughts and concerns in order to channel her higher power. This act of *clearing* is the means of entering the transpersonal state and is similar to how mediums enter into a trance.

HEALING TOUCH AND EDUCATION

One of the key differences between Healing Touch and Therapeutic Touch is their educational model. Therapeutic Touch has a very limited instruction period while Healing Touch International requires nurses to takes a five-year course before their international board grants them a license. It is interesting to note that many of their courses are of a spiritual nature, rather than a therapeutic nature. Some of the courses are: *Location and Function of the Chakras*; *Healing Techniques: Spiral Meditation, Mind Clearing and Reading The Auras*; *The Practice of Hara Alignment*; *Chelation Therapy*; *Etheric Template Clearing*; and *Development of Higher Sense Perception*. This final course is prerequisite for advancing past year three of the program.[71]

There is also assigned reading for each course. The required reading assignments include the writings of the leading figures of Theosophy. These

---

[71] The Healing Beyond Borders HTI Healing Touch Certificate Program https://www.healingbeyondborders.org/index.php/education (Accessed October 15, 2022).

include Madam Helena Blavatsky, Annie Besant, Charles Leadbeater and Alice Bailey. Allan Kardec, Father of Spiritism is also part of the list. Other contemporary religious writings are part of the reading assignments as well. The works of Barbara Brennan, Deepak Chopra, Larry Dossey and the Dalai Lama are also part of the core reading requirements. In this, we see the influence of Theosophy, Buddhism, Hinduism and Spiritism on the educational model of Healing Touch. The entire description of courses and reading requirements is viewable at *www.Healing Touch.org*.

MEDICAL ANALYSIS OF HEALING TOUCH

Brent Bauer, MD concludes from the Mayo Clinic's study of Healing Touch that "Proponents of Healing Touch claim to be effective in treating stress-related problems, allergies, heart conditions, high blood pressure and chronic pain. So far, there is no hard data to confirm this.

Many small studies of Healing Touch have suggested it is effective in treating a variety of conditions. One recent report states that participants of seven studies had positive outcomes, while those in three other studies showed no effect at all. However, the control group in another study fared better than those who received Healing Touch therapy.

We recognize that people perceive health benefits from Healing Touch. Some people find the therapy is relaxing and certainly, relaxation is good for your health. However, beyond relaxation, there is limited scientific evidence that Healing Touch improves health. Because of the low risk involved in Healing Touch, whether to try the therapy is up to you, based on how closely it fits with your personal beliefs".[72]

INTERVIEW WITH A HEALING TOUCH PRACTITIONER

Deborah Larrimore, RN, BSN, LMBT, CHTP/I is director of "The Healing Touch Education Program For Complementary and Integrative Medicine" at Wake Forest University Baptist Medical Center in Winston-Salem, North Carolina. Deborah was kind enough to grant the author a telephone interview concerning her practice of Healing Touch as an

---

[72] Bauer, Brent MD. (2007). *Book of Alternative Medicine.* New York, New York: Time Inc. pp. 110.

educator, practitioner, and director at the medical center. Deborah travels across the United States speaking in a variety of settings. She gave the author the opportunity to ask several questions concerning the spirituality of Healing Touch and her practice as a Healing Touch therapist. This is not a verbatim interview, but is a compilation of Deborah's thoughts.

1. *What are some of the differences between Healing Touch, and Therapeutic Touch?*

Deborah: Therapeutic Touch focuses on the bio field and movement through the air. It uses the therapist's hands in no distinct pattern or place in order to practice Therapeutic Touch. Whereas Dolores Krieger could not see the energy that she was inducing, Dora Kunz was able to see the energy field points of congestion and the individual's aura.

I believe that all of us as children can see the bio energy field or aura. However, as we grow older, pressures of society block us from seeing this field. Biblically, we see this field represented in many paintings by halos around the heads of the various characters. Therapeutic Touch derives from a collection of various healers throughout the country and around the world.

> *"I believe that all of us as children can see the bio energy field or aura".*

Healing Touch does not see itself as a cure, or about a cure, but instead promotes itself as a sense of well-being. In my work with hospice, many patients died and healing was not complete. However, they had a sense of calmness and relaxation and passed away peacefully rather than in a state of anxiety and agitation.

Therapeutic Touch relates to the human energy system including the human bio field. These bio-fields or energy centers are called chakras and meridian lines. Healing Touch, on the other hand, is somewhat concerned about the bio field chakras, and meridians. However, it has a much broader basis to its practice.

One of the key differences between Healing Touch and Therapeutic Touch is that Healing Touch has become a standardized practice consisting of verifiable techniques. There is a curriculum, a teaching process, a common language and level of understanding. When completed, it results in certification by an international board of review. There are five levels of study requiring at least three years of instruction and a year of mentorship under a nurse practitioner, including 1,000 hours of supervision.

Interestingly with Healing Touch, a physician can order standardized treatments, dictate them and nurses can implement them. Nurses from the next shift who to take care of the same patient, will know exactly what treatments are complete and which treatments remain. Everything is standardized.

2.   *Delores Krieger bases much of the spirituality connected with Therapeutic Touch around Eastern religions such as Hinduism, as well as the practice of African Animism. Do you use of any particular non-Western religious practices?*

Deborah: In Healing Touch, we encourage people to connect with their own religious path and not to try to convert them to another form of spirituality or belief. We teach a spiritual course about connecting with their Higher Power or the Divine Other. Healing Touch is a vehicle to all and every religion.

In my work with hospice, we support each person's individual religious view. Unlike Dolores Krieger, Healing Touch does not address the issue of communication with inanimate things. Of course, every teacher or practitioner has a sense of autonomy and may share some of their own beliefs during their practice of Healing Touch.

My classes in Healing Touch help people to connect to their homes and families to experience a spiritual awakening. Recently, I had a Chinese doctor who came to class who was an atheist. During a Healing Touch session, *her mom and her dad came to her* and she had a conversion experience from atheism to spiritual reality.

3.   *You stated that you have had a number of "mystical" experiences during Healing Touch sessions in which you have sensed or have even visually seen deceased loved ones, angels and spirit guides. Could you relate a couple of these?*

Deborah: I do not refer to the guides that I encounter during Healing Touch sessions as spirit guides. I have seen several forms or outlines of a person and I have one photograph that I will e-mail you a copy of that pictures a gathering of angels. Now you cannot make out the distinct characterization of any particular angel, but instead you can see bright lights surrounding the individual that bear a striking resemblance to the biblical picture of angels.

The case I am thinking about was about a man in hospice who was dying and who owned a dog that was also dying. This man did not want to die before his dog passed away because he did not want the dog to experience that kind of loss. Because of this, he stopped treatment on his dog. As his dog lay in bed with him, he had one of the nurses take a picture of him and his dog. When the photos came back, there were pictures of angels, beings of light, standing around the man and his dog. You can easily tell they were some sort of life forms. I prefer to call them angels.

My father also experienced a serious illness, where he suffered from an aortic aneurysm. I could not see anyone, but felt the presence of many of my deceased relatives including my mother. I knew who was there, and who was not there in my father's illness. I do not believe there were any spirit guides there, but I do believe my family had gathered around the bedside.

In another instance, I was with a friend of mine in Mobile, Alabama, whose father was a doctor. His name was Bill. He had died some years ago, and now his daughter, my friend, was dying. While I was with her, a word came across my mind; it was the word "Pumpkin". Somehow, I knew this word was significant in so I asked my friend if the word Pumpkin meant anything special to her. She said that Pumpkin was her father's pet name for her ever since she was a little girl. Knowing that he was with her, gave her a sense of peace that she never could have had in any other way. Of course, these are subjective experiences that cannot be proven but I know they are true because as I have seen them repeatedly in my practice.

4. *Since you told me that your Dad is a minister, I am curious how you integrate your Christian upbringing with the mystical experiences that you have had.*

Deborah: it is not difficult at all. I grew up in the Moravian church, which incorporates healing services and the laying on of hands. I participate in these practices but I do not go into a detailed explanation of my own beliefs. I believe that Healing Touch blends perfectly with Christianity and promotes Christ's teaching concerning his ministry of healing.

5. *I recently received an e-mail from a doctor who felt that the basis of all touch healing was the existence of natural electromagnetic fields both in the body and in the universe around us. I would like your viewpoint concerning this.*

Deborah: I think that is an excellent concept because science shows us what happens. It shows us what happens physically, it also shows us what happens spiritually. I do not know if you are aware of this or not but frequencies and electricity are measurable in hertz. Everyone's hands give off the same electrical charge measured in hertz. It is the same frequency used in medical treatments. So yes, we do have electromagnetic fields.

I am a Reiki practitioner as well. Sometimes I participate in a ceremony of empowerment through the practice of Attunement. However, I could not agree with it because I could see no scientific evidence for it. I think measuring bio-fields and their electrical field is a much better approach. Part of teaching must be pure science.

> *"Science plus intentionality, or the emotions, act as a conduit for connecting with a higher power that attracts the presence of God, angels, and our loved ones who are deceased".*

The spiritual component makes a difference too. Without it the mechanical aspect does not work. Hertz are just hertz without intentionality. There must be goodwill, compassion, and love in order to create the flow of frequency. Science plus intentionality, or the emotions, act as a conduit for connecting with a higher power that attracts the presence of God, angels, and our loved ones who are deceased. I think Carl Jung said, "Learn theory the best you can but put it aside and use touch as the miracle that connects with the soul."

The reason that I practice Healing Touch is because I believe God called me as a nurse to use Healing Touch to minister to the patients that I care for. I have seen that it is effective in meeting the needs of my patients and touches their lives spiritually. I find this very fulfilling and spiritually rewarding. I am fulfilling my mission in life.

SUMMARY AND CONCLUSIONS

Healing Touch calls itself an alternative medical therapy. Although the practice claims a scientific basis in the field of physics and electromagnetism, the world's foremost medical institutions cannot substantiate this idea. As with other "touch therapies", Healing Touch claims a rational and logical basis. Nevertheless, as we have found, it has nothing in common with the rationalistic logic based Western ideas of medicine. Instead, it is firmly rooted in Eastern religion. Healing Touch borrows the idea of a Vital Life Force permeating all around us, from Buddhists pantheistic beliefs. It also borrows polytheistic religious healing modalities such as Ayurvedic Medicine and Yoga and incorporates them into its practice.

Healing Touch does not stop in just borrowing religious ideas from other cultures; it also incorporates Spiritism and the occult as part of its methodology. Class curriculum used in the Healing Touch educational program offers training in energizing the *chakras,* use of *hara lines,* how to read *auras,* and how to *channel spirits, angels and other figures* by developing the student's *higher sense perception.*

During Healing Touch sessions, therapists practice *clairvoyance, clairaudience* and *necromancy* by *channeling* spirits, angels and deceased family members. They use these contacts to gain information about their clients, the nature of the illness as well as guidance on how to promote healing. Conclusion: Healing Touch is not an alternative medical therapy. The best medical minds in the country say so. It is not effective since studies argue this point convincingly. Healing Touch is a religious and esoteric practice that looks to Eastern religion and the dark arts as its basis. These things they freely admit.

Christians beware, especially those involved in the medical field. Those like nurse Deborah Larrimore, are blind and will try to convince you that Healing Touch augments the healing ministry of Christ. Practioner's will state that God has called them to do His work "work". There is nothing further from the truth. God's work is the work of Jesus Christ through the Holy Spirit. Even though Healing Touch therapists may be from conservation religious backgrounds and the homes of ministers, nevertheless watch out, "*the poison of asps is under their lips*" (Romans 3:13). Just because Healing Touch can baptize itself in Christian terminology does not make it Christian. Satan is the great Deceiver. 2 Timothy 3:13 warns us, *"evil men and seducers shall wax worse and worse, deceiving, and being deceived"*.

When it is recommended that you receive training in Healing Touch, or if you are asked to receive treatment, do not give Satan a foothold. Healing Touch is not alternative medicine, it is not an extension of the healing ministry of Christ, it is an Eastern and occultic practice and as believers, we should have nothing to do with it.

STUDY QUESTIONS

A LIE CALLED HEALING TOUCH

1. How are Healing Touch and Therapeutic Touch Different from one another?

2. Who was Janet Mentgen and how did she develop Healing Touch?

3. What are the stages in a Healing Touch session?

4. How does Mentgen attempt to use science (electricity and electromagnetism) to give credibility to Healing Touch?

5. How does Hinduism contribute to the spirituality of Healing Touch?

6. What occult practices are used by Healing Touch practitioners?

7. How does the occult influence the education system of so important to Healing touch?

8. What insight can be gained and important conclusions can Christians make from the interview with Deborah Larimore?

9.   Why is Healing Touch incompatible with Christianity?

10. How should Christians respond to claims that Healing Touch is Christian?

CHAPTER 9

CHALLENGES FACING NURSING

CHAPTER 9
CHALLENGES FACING NURSING

*"Eskimo: "If I did not know about God and sin,
would I go to hell?"*

Priest: "No, not if you did not know."

Eskimo: "Then why did you tell me?"

— Annie Dillard

THE HISTORY OF NURSING

Nursing developed in various forms in every culture. Originally, nurses were either a *wet nurse* or a *dry nurse,* referring to those who performed breast-feeding as opposed to those who cared for sick children. In the 15th century, the concept of nursing evolved into the idea of "looking after or advising another" and included the care of adults. Nursing continued to develop in the broadest sense of the word, and referred to promoting "quality of life".

Before the founding of modern nursing, nuns and the military provided nursing-like services. The religious and military roots of modern nursing remain today in many countries. For example, in the United Kingdom, senior female nurses are known as "sisters". It was during times of war that a significant development in nursing history occurred. English nurse, *Florence Nightingale,* worked to improve conditions of soldiers in the Crimean War. She laid the foundation of professional nursing with the principles summarized in the book *Notes on Nursing.*

Other important nurses in developing the profession include Mary Seacole, who also worked as a nurse in the Crimea. Agnes Elizabeth Jones and Linda Richards established quality-nursing schools in the United States and Japan. Richards was officially America's first trained nurse, graduating in 1873 from the *New England Hospital for Women and Children* in Boston. Modern education offers various degrees in nursing and publishes NUMEROUS journals to broaden the knowledge base of the profession. Nurses occupy key management roles within health services and hold research posts at universities.

We must take a moment and celebrate the role of nursing. Nurses are among the best gifts to people everywhere. They are compassionate, caring and kind almost to a fault. Anyone that has been a patient has come to feel the nurse who cared for them was a Godsend and they do not know what they would have done without them. Some people even look on nurses as "angels of mercy". No one should ever read the information contained within these pages and think that professional nurses are seen less than in a positive light. Some nurses may mistakenly tread down the dangerous path of touch therapies and alternative medicine, but they often do so unknowingly, motivated by their love for people. Nurses are and continue to be among the best of God's creatures.

FLORENCE NIGHTINGALE

Florence Nightingale was born into an upper class, well-connected British family at Florence, Grand Duchy of Tuscany, and named after the city of her birth. On February 7th 1837, not long before her 17th birthday, something happened that would change her life forever. "God spoke to me", she wrote, "and called me to His service". Inspired by what she took as a divine calling, Florence announced her decision to enter nursing in 1845. She did this despite the intense anger and distress of her family, especially her mother. She rebelled against the expected role for a woman of her status to become a wife and mother. Nightingale worked hard to educate herself in the art and science of nursing, despite the restrictive societal code for affluent young English women.

Florence Nightingale's most famous contribution came during the Crimean War. The war became her focus when reports began to filter back to Britain about the horrific conditions for the wounded. On October 21, 1854, she and a staff of 38 volunteer nurses, under the protection of Sidney Herbert, arrived in Turkey. She and her nurses found wounded soldiers poorly cared for by an overworked medical staff in the face of official indifference. Medicines were scarce and hygiene barely existed. Mass infections were common, many of them fatal. Also, there was no equipment to process food for the patients.

"Notice the primary reason that Florence Nightingale entered the field of nursing was because she felt that God was calling her to a life of service to care for the sick".

During the Crimean campaign, Florence Nightingale gained the nickname *"The Lady with the Lamp"*, stemming from a phrase in a report in *The Times*. The phrase became popular through Henry Wadsworth Longfellow's 1857 poem *"Santa Filomena"*:

Lo! in that hour of misery,
A lady with a lamp I see,
Pass through the glimmering gloom,
And flit from room to room.

By 1859, Nightingale had £45,000 at her disposal from the Nightingale Fund to set up the Nightingale Training School at St. Thomas' Hospital. It is still part of the Florence Nightingale School of Nursing and Midwifery. Nightingale wrote *Notes on Nursing*, published in 1860. This slim 136-page book served as the cornerstone of the curriculum at the Nightingale School and at other nursing schools as they were established. *Notes on Nursing* is a popular text and continues to be a classic introduction to nursing. Nightingale spent the rest of her life promoting, establishing and developing the nursing profession and organizing it into its modern form.[73]

Notice the primary reason that Florence Nightingale entered the field of nursing was because *she felt that God was calling her to a life of service* to care for the sick. While today, nurses do not often cite a sense of divine call as the reason they enter nursing as a profession, the number one reason they do become a nurse is that *they want to help others.*

NURSING THEORY

Nursing theory is the term given to the body of knowledge that supports nursing practice. Florence Nightingale essentially developed the first theory of nursing. In their professional education, nurses will study interrelated subjects that apply to the practical setting. This knowledge stems from formal classroom teaching to the practice of clinical skills. Nursing is many things to many people. Most agree that nursing is a science involving people, environment and process, fueled by a vision of transcendence about healthcare. Theories vary from discipline to discipline depending on what fields of care the nurse may be working in. 90% of all Nursing theories have come into existence in the last 20 years.

THE MEDICAL HOME THEORY

An understanding of medical theory *is crucial in comprehending the expanding role of nurses in integrative alternative medicine.* As we examine medical theory, it will also help us understand how the role of nursing is changing the face of spiritual care.

Medical Home, also known as Patient-Centered Medical Home (PCMH), is defined as "an approach to providing comprehensive primary care that promotes partnerships between individual patients, and their personal physicians, and when appropriate, the patient's family." The provisions of Medical Home allow better access to health care, increased patient satisfaction, and improved health. The influence of Medical Home is evident when listening to the jargon spoken in hospital hallways and

---

[73]   Bostridge, Mark. (2008). *Florence Nightingale: The Woman and Her Legend.* London: Viking. P. 82.

patient's rooms every day. Patients and their families will overhear doctors and nurses discussing *evidence based practice, patient centered care* and *outcome based medicine.* Each of these terms stems from the practice of the Medical Home Theory.

ELEMENTS OF THE MEDICAL HOME THEORY

In 2007, the American Academy of Family Physicians, the American Academy of Pediatrics, the American College of Physicians, and the American Osteopathic Association — the leading physician organizations in the United States — released the "Joint Principles of Patient-Centered Medical Home." The principles are:

- **Personal physician**: "each patient has a right to an ongoing relationship with a personal physician trained to provide first contact and continuous and comprehensive care."
- **Physician directed medical practice**: "the personal physician leads a team of individuals at the practice level who collectively take responsibility for the ongoing care of patients."
- **Whole person orientation**: "the personal physician is responsible for providing for all the patient's health care needs and taking responsibility for appropriately arranging care with other qualified professionals."
- **Care is coordinated and integrated**, across specialists, hospitals, home health agencies, and nursing homes.
- **Quality and safety** are integral by a care planning process, evidence-based medicine, clinical decision-support tools, performance measurement, active participation of patients in decision-making, information technology, a voluntary recognition process, quality improvement activities, and other measures.
- **Enhanced access** to care is available (e.g., via "open scheduling, expanded hours and new options for communication").
- **Payment** "appropriately recognizes the added value provided to patients who have a patient-centered medical home." For instance, payment should reflect the value of "work that falls outside of the face-to-face visit," should "support adoption and use of health

information technology for quality improvement," and should "recognize case mix differences in the patient population being treated within the practice."[74]

IMPLICATIONS OF THE MEDICAL HOME THEORY ON NURSING

Fascinatingly, implementation of the Medical Home Theory has broadened the role of nursing in providing alternative care. As a result, some nurses unwittingly become practitioners of treatments that contradict their faith in Christ. On the other hand, there are also those who fully understand the spiritual basis of touch therapies and with great vigor, pursue spreading their teaching as widely as possible. These individuals are spiritually dangerous. Jesus said, *"Fear him which is able to destroy both soul and body in hell"* (Matthew 10:28).

Three aspects of the Medical Home Theory are primarily responsible for the shift in medicine that has opened the door to touch therapies. The first is, *"integrated care"*. The idea behind coordinated care has led to developing the *Interdisciplinary Team*. This team consists of doctors, nurses, pharmacists, therapists, social workers, chaplains and all others who provide care to the patient.

"The bedside nurse has the greatest access to the patient".

Now, not only is the doctor responsible for the patient's care, but every member of the team has a shared responsibility in caring for the patient. Another facet of the Interdisciplinary Team is that all disciplines share one another's responsibilities. A chaplain may discover that a patient's spiritual concerns are affecting their medical treatment and will collaborate with the doctor, nurse or any other team member to redirect care. Similarly, a doctor may collaborate with the social worker to provide care for a particular patient.

---

[74] Hernandez-Shea, Doty Beal. *Closing The Divide: How Medical Home Promotes Equity In Health Care.* New York: The Commonwealth Fund, 2007

Interestingly, *the bedside nurse has the greatest access to the patient.* She is also the only member of the team to provide around the clock care. In many respects, *she becomes responsible to provide or make sure care from each discipline is available.* In lieu of team member's presence, she may gather information for the social worker, counsel the patient, or pray on their behalf. Coordinated Care has heaped much responsibility on the nurse.

The second aspect of the Medical Home Theory that has affected the role of nursing is, *Whole Person Orientation.* One of the great complaints about medicine has been the failure of doctors and nurses to see the patient as an individual with needs, concerns and fears. For example, the person in room 323 is not "the heart case" his name is "John". Whole person orientation recognizes "John" as an individual whose needs include addressing not only the illness, but his emotional and spiritual welfare as well.

Challenging nurses, is the need to see their patients through this new paradigm and attempt to meet their needs "holistically". As a result, nurses have begun to take on many new roles. Unfortunately, nurses lack adequate education to provide some of these cares. Nurses do not have a social work degree, nor do they have a counseling degree, and they are not seminary graduates either. Nevertheless, they must assume these roles periodically.

Commendably, nurses are willing to assume a variety of roles. Nurses are compassionate, caring people who strive to do their best to care for their patients. It is admirable that many are willing to go the extra mile to provide care. However, it is important to notice the nurse's role has changed. It is also important in our discussion of touch therapies, to notice that she now must provide spiritual and emotional support in addition to physical cares.

The third aspect of the Medical Home Theory that has far-reaching implications for nurses is the idea of *Enhanced Access.* Enhanced Access means that patients are to have access to all modalities or treatments that is possible to give them. This is a positive idea but it has broadened into dangerous territory.

In the area of medical care, *Enhanced Access* has come to mean not only providing every needed conventional intervention, but also every alternative and complementary intervention necessary. This includes patient access to all forms of alternative therapies, even the spiritually toxic ones we have addressed. It also means including all forms of spirituality.

The face of medical and spiritual care in our hospitals and hospices is rapidly changing. The lines between medicine and religion have blurred. In a later chapter, we will see that pastoral care has become impotent. Caught in the middle of this confusion stands the nurse. Hearing only half-truths about alternative and spiritual care, they are surprised when they understand the full scope of what is taking place around them. Yet according to medical theory, it is their job to provide these cares.

UNDERSTANDING HOLISTIC NURSING

On the surface, holistic nursing sounds like a well-balanced approach to providing patient care. In their philosophy, the American Holistic Nurses Association states that," Holistic nursing defines itself as all nursing practices that has healing the whole person as its goal." A holistic nurse is a registered and licensed nurse who takes a mind-body-spirit-emotion approach to the practice of traditional nursing. Holistic nurses encourage their patients to take responsibility for their own individual wellness through positive lifestyle changes and daily self-care. Holistic nurses listen to their patients and empower them with the knowledge they need to live healthier, more balanced lives".[75]

DEVELOPMENT OF HOLISTIC MEDICINE

Ancient healing traditions, as far back as 5,000 years ago in India and China, stressed living a healthy way of life in harmony with nature. Socrates (4th century BC) warned against treating only one part of the body, "for the part can never be well unless the whole is well." Jan Christiaan Smuts introduced the term holism in 1926. She used it as a way of viewing living things as "entities greater than the sum of their parts." It was not until the 1970s that holistic medicine became a common phrase in our modern vocabulary.

Holistic ideas fell temporarily out of favor in Western societies during the 20th Century. Scientific medical advances had created a dramatic shift in ideas about health. Doctors and researchers understood that germs are the outside sources causing disease. Restoring health meant killing

---

[75]   What is Holistic Nursing? https://www.ahna.org/About-Us/What-is-Holistic-Nursing (Accessed October 15, 2022).

microscopic invaders with synthesized drugs. People believed that they could get away with unhealthy lifestyle choices, and modern medicine would "fix" them as problems developed.

"The holistic health lifestyle is regaining popularity each year".

However, for some conditions, medical cures have proven as debilitating as the disease. In addition, many chronic conditions do not respond to scientific medical treatments. In looking for other options, people are turning to holistic approaches of health and healing. The holistic health lifestyle is regaining popularity each year, as holistic principles offer practical options to meet the growing desire to enjoy a sense of vitality and well-being.

THE AMERICAN HOLISTIC NURSES ASSOCIATION

As the definitive voice for holistic nursing, the American Holistic Nurses Association (AHNA) promotes the education of nurses, healthcare professionals and the public concerning holistic medicine. AHNA is a non-profit membership association serving more than 4,100 members and 160 local chapters and networks across the U.S. and abroad. In December of 2006, because of the efforts of AHNA, holistic nursing became an "official nursing specialty" by the American Nurses Association.

AHNA serves as a bridge between conventional healthcare and complementary and alternative healing practices. As health care professionals, holistic nurses integrate complementary and alternative modalities into clinical practice to treat the whole person. They view healing as a partnership between the patient and their practitioner.

As a member of the National Center for Complementary and Alternative Medicine (NCCAM), AHNA recognizes a multitude of alternative healing modalities including those mentioned earlier. These include *whole body systems* (homeopathy, osteopathy); *manipulation practices* (acupuncture and acupressure, massage, chiropractic medicine,); *mind-body based medicine* (hypnotherapy, meditation, yoga, t'ai chi, and *energy therapies* (Reiki, Healing Touch, and Therapeutic Touch).

The mission of the AHNA is to advance holistic nursing by providing continuing education to nurses. Their goal is to help improve the health care workplace. The AHNA does this by educating professionals and the public about holistic nursing, integrative health care, and promoting research and scholarship in the field of holistic nursing.

One can easily see the AHNA has an agenda. It is not hiding or camouflaging it in any way. The association exists to "educate nurses about alternative therapies, promoting them to the public, and adopting these therapies into mainline medicine". According to their web site *www. ahana.org,* this includes touch therapies. The AHNA is the single largest proponent of alternative medicine and its therapies in the U. S. Their goal is to penetrate the field of nursing with alternative and complementary practices. Christian nurses must be aware of this organization.

ALTERNATIVE MEDICINE IN HOSPICE

Hospice programs throughout the country are hotbeds for insidious alternative health care practices. The Hospice and Palliative Care Nurses Association (HPNA) has resolved to support the use of alternative therapies in hospice. They have done this despite the fact that the best medical institutions in this country have concluded the therapies are ineffective and have no benefit. However it does recognize that there *is a lack of empirical evidence at a high level.* Anecdotal reports suggest that professional nurses who use these modalities believe that patients experience an increased sense of comfort and well-being after receiving these types of therapy. Nevertheless, they can point to no objective facts. HPNA's commitment to the use of alternative therapies is clear in its position statement.

Position Statement

This is the position of the HPNA Board of Directors:

- Acknowledge the increasing popularity and use of complementary therapies and recognize that this trend has important implications for nursing practice, education, and research.
- Recognize that many complementary therapies provide a holistic approach to managing symptoms and promoting wellness at the

end of life. The holistic approach is consistent with nursing's historical and philosophical methods of practice.

- Recognize the current and potential role of complementary therapies in the amelioration of symptoms and enhancement of quality of life for patients with life-limiting illness.
- Assure that hospice and palliative nurses have sufficient access to resources about these therapies to guide patients in making informed decisions regarding their care and to incorporate these therapies into a comprehensive plan of care.
- Support basic and continuing nursing education focusing on complementary therapies for patients with life-limiting illnesses.
- Support and encourage the competent practice of complementary therapies for promoting holistic end-of-life care.
- Affirm that some complementary therapies are within the scope of nursing practice.
- Promote regulatory and legislative clarification regarding the scope of nursing practice as it relates to complementary therapies.
- Support safe, rigorous, and ethically sound research that examines the efficacy, costs, and adverse effects of complementary therapies.
- Educate nurses regarding State and Federal regulations on CAM.
- Support the use of licensed and certified CAM therapists in the delivery of these service
- Acknowledge the impact cultural diversity has on CAM in America.[76]

HPNA recognizes that the greatest asset it has to implement alternative therapies is the hospice nurse. They state that nursing care for those with life-limiting illnesses has long embraced the individual as a whole, encompassing the physical, mental, emotional, and spiritual dimensions of care. Therefore, *nursing is a natural fit for the use of alternative and complementary therapies.* Some of the more common CAM modalities used by nurses include acupressure, aromatherapy, biofeedback, guided

---

[76] Complementary and Alternative Medicine In Hospice https://pubmed.ncbi.nlm.nih.gov/15510566/ (Accessed December 3, 2022).

imagery, healing presence, meditation, relaxation, Reiki and Therapeutic Touch and Healing Touch.[77]

A Hospice Story

Peter, a Registered Nurse, had recently joined the staff of a local hospice house. His caring manner and cheerful attitude had already made him popular with the residents. One day a chaplain happened to walk into a room where Peter was attending to a resident and found him lighting some incense sticks that were in a jar. At the same time, he noticed a crystal hanging from the light above the bed. Later as he spoke with Peter about this, he discovered that Peter was eager to incorporate a number of alternative therapies into his nursing care. Some of the proposed interventions and the philosophies behind them were incompatible with the chaplain's ethos and the beliefs of most staff and residents. The chaplain brought Peter's behavior to the attention of the Director of the Hospice who quickly told him that his concern was inappropriate as hospice supports all forms of alternative care.

HOW NURSES CAN RESPOND TO ALTERNATIVE MEDICINE

Please notice that hospice nurses are particularly vulnerable to exposure to alternative practices that contradict their faith. This is because hospice patients have exhausted all medical interventions and have failed to recover. Compassionate, loving nurses know this and are willing to try additional therapies that promise hope and help.

During a recent session of a Parish Nursing training course, Christian nurses were surprised and even shocked to hear about the spiritual roots of some alternative therapies they were to engage in. Some of them had already received the training. A flurry of anxious conversation buzzed about the room. Some were subtlety prodded to take Reiki or Healing Touch courses. Others had already taken initial training in these or other integrative therapies and felt that they had unknowingly betrayed their faith in Christ. Bewildered, many of the nurses did not know how they should respond in their work environments.

---

[77]   Ibid.

"Nursing is a natural fit for the use of alternative and complementary therapies".

As a nurse or other healthcare professional, it is important to learn about the spiritualities connected with various alternative therapies. As the trend in health care continues, it will not be long until management confronts you with choices about taking part in alternative care. It may be costly to object because of your faith. If you choose not to participate in training, there may be subtle reparations for your choice. It may be something as simple as feeling that you are falling out of favor with your employer. It may also be more serious and affect your employment if administrators believe that you are unable to provide non-judgmental care because of your Christian views.

The question remains, "How should Christian nurses respond to the practice of alternative medicine in their work environment?" The first issue might be, "How do they affect you and to what extent"? Are spiritually harmful therapies simply part of your work environment, or are they a threat to your personal faith? A second issue that might come up is, "In what ways are you influenced to make the therapy part of your nursing practice"? This can be a serious question for the committed Christian. The third issue could be, "How is the Holy Spirit convicting you to respond to harmful alternative therapies as a nurse?"

At times, Christ wants us to be salt and light where we are. At other times, he tells us "to *flee the appearance of evil*"(1 Thessalonians 5:22). Jesus said, "*My sheep know my voice*" (John 10:27). We must be in tune with the Shepherd's voice so we can clearly discern what he is saying to us in our workplace.

Some nurses may realize that their faith is on the line where they are working at and they need to make a change. They may need to shift to another department, move from a hospice to the hospital, a physician's office, a clinic or a care center. God may have another form of ministry that He wants them to fulfill elsewhere.

Other nurses could find that the use of alternative care is pervasive throughout their health system. In this case, God may call you to make a radical decision to leave your employer. Other opportunities exist which will not conflict with your faith. Some nurses have chosen to become a parish nurse in their local church. Others have found exciting ministries in Christian camping, schools or education. Wherever you are, know this axiom is true, *"God never closes one door without opening another"*. God will always have a place for you to use your gifts and your talents. The Bible assures us that *"the gifts and calling of God are without repentance"*. (Romans 11:29).

A CHRISTIAN PERSPECTIVE

Christian nurses are finding themselves working is an environment that is becoming increasingly hostile to their faith. In an article questioning teaching Therapeutic Touch in nursing schools, the writers concluded that Therapeutic Touch is a religious practice. They state that it is unsuitable for Christians to use without "seriously compromising their faith and potentially endangering their relationship with God". They offer an argument that, if followed to its logical conclusion, suggests that any practice that arises from belief systems opposing Christianity may be detrimental.[78]

RNs are the largest healthcare occupation in the U.S. The Bureau of Labor and Statistics estimates there are about 2.3 million registered nurses in the U.S. 1,480,400 identify themselves as Christian. Christian nurses should never feel alone as they try to sort through the area of alternative medicine. Thousands of Christians, who work as nurses must learn how to cope with alternative care. Just as Florence Nightingale was true to God's call on her life despite family and social pressures, so nurses today must find ways to fulfill God's call in their lives that does not violate their faith.

---

[78] Faith Community Nursing: Scope and Standards of Practice, https://www.nursingworld.org/nurses-books/faith-community-nursing-scope-and-standards-of-practice-3rd-edition/ (Accessed November 8, 2022).

STUDY QUESTIONS

CHALLENGES FACING NURSING

1. Why did Florence Nightingale want to become a nurse?

2. What is the Medical Home Theory?

3. What are three implications of the Medical Home Theory on Nurses?

4. What role does Holistic Nursing play in alternative medicine and touch therapies?

5. What is the position of Hospice on the use of alternative medicine and touch therapies?

6. What challenges do Christian nurses and other health care professionals face in view of the growing incursion of touch therapies in their work place?

7. What advice is offered to Christian health care professionals who are trying to integrate their faith and their work?

8. What dangers exist for Christian nurses in work environments with toxic forms of alternative medicine?

9. What comfort is offered at the end of this chapter?

CHAPTER 10

THE CULT CALLED SPIRITUAL CARE

CHAPTER 10
THE CULT CALLED SPIRITUAL CARE

"And then she understood the devilish cunning of the enemies' plan. By mixing a little truth with it they had made their lie far stronger."

— C. S. Lewis

In the past, if you were in a Catholic hospital, a priest or a nun would provide your spiritual care. In a Methodist, Baptist or Lutheran hospital, chaplains from those denominations would provide for your spiritual care respectively. Even in our large tertiary hospitals today, many churches sponsor denominational chaplains to meet the spiritual needs of their patients. Nevertheless, this is becoming less true with the passage of time. Today's chaplains may be from most any denominational background or have little or no theological training at all. In addition, a growing number of chaplains are not Christian but represent various religious traditions including Buddhism, Islam, and some are members of cult groups. These chaplains may offer to pray with you, but the god they are praying to is not God the Father, nor His Son Jesus Christ.

A disturbing characteristic of present-day chaplaincy is the capacity that chaplains have for acting as *"spiritual chameleons"*. They blend in with whatever spiritual background the patient does or does not have. Required by their job constraints they must assure patients that their beliefs are as valid as any other. They will tell the patient there are *"many pathways that lead to God"*.

Most chaplains are still Christian ministers and are loving and caring professionals. Despite this, their health care institutions force them to betray their faith in Christ, as well as their personal integrity as they provide spiritual care to patients. These institutions mandate the content and means the chaplain may use to give spiritual care. Some chaplains feel torn between professional dictates and their own faith. The question is "why has this happened and how has it come about"?

CHANGES IN SPIRITUAL CARE

The nature of pastoral care has changed in the health environment over the past few years. In fact, "pastoral care" has been renamed "spiritual care". If you walk into the chaplain's office at most any hospital, you will see a sign identifying the department as "spiritual care". This subtle change is telling. Somewhere along the way, spiritual care divorced itself from God and faith. This differentiation is evident in health care's definition of spirituality and religion. A good definition appears in the Hospice and Palliative Care Association's position statement. It defines "*religion* as a group of beliefs, a belief system or a faith tradition concerning the supernatural, sacred or divine and the moral codes, practices, values, institutions and rituals associated with such belief. *Spirituality* is that which gives a person meaning, value, purpose and worth in life. It consists of the individual's ties with experiences of transcendence, wonder, awe, joy, and connection to nature, self, and others. It strives to make the patient's experience meaningful and to maintain hope when illness strikes. "From a Christian perspective, the new spirituality is more about an *emotional connection* and the comfort it brings rather than stemming from faith in God. In fact, spirituality may even be devoid of God altogether".[79]

> *"Somewhere along the way, spiritual care divorced itself from God and faith".*

Another important aspect of the new spirituality is that it is inclusive of all faith traditions, and sees each as equally valid. This form of spiritual care values the uniqueness of each person by recognizing and honoring an

---

[79]   HPNA Value, Policy, and Position Statements https://advancingexpertcare.org/position-statements/ (Accessed October 15, 2022).

individual's beliefs, values, practices and rituals. It sees itself as open to the full discussion, expression and experiences of each one's beliefs. This form of spiritual care may seem appropriate in the health care setting until we understand that it is diametrically opposed to true spirituality integral to faith in Christ. Jesus said, "*I am the Way, the Truth and the Life; no man comes to the Father but by me* (John 14:6).

It is not difficult to see that a new spiritual practice has arisen in health care. Some might even say that it is *cult-like*. That new spirituality attempts to cloak itself in the trappings of Christianity by hiring Christian chaplains to provide spiritual care. Nevertheless, chaplains cannot provide Bible-based counsel *unless specifically requested by a patient*. Instead, they must uphold the spiritual myth fabricated by hospital administrations and government agencies on pains of losing their jobs.

Because of this, health systems everywhere have redefined spirituality to mean 1.) Spirituality excludes religion and ultimately excludes Christ. 2.) Instead, it offers a spiritual belief in the universal equity of all faiths or lack of faith. 3.) It promotes inclusion and diversity denying the reality that there, "*Neither is there salvation in any other: for there is none other name under heaven given among men, whereby we must be saved except through the name of Jesus*" (Acts 4:12). 4.) It is a false faith, as false as any cult in existence today. 5.) It denies the divinity of Jesus Christ, His sacrificial death on the Cross, the need for repentance, God's offer of forgiveness for sin, and salvation in Christ alone. The "cult of health care" even hires its own clergy to staff and promote its belief system. Some may scoff at the idea that a cult has entered the practice of health care. Nevertheless, scrutiny shows that health care has its own belief system that demands uniformity and threatens to terminate chaplains who fail to comply. These facts are all characteristics of a cult.

WHY SPIRITUAL CARE HAS CHANGED

Spiritual care has lost touch with its pastoral roots, and become secular. The names of denominationally sponsored hospitals may still identify them with a particular church. Nevertheless, health care institutions are primarily businesses with CEO's and a board of directors. Administrators have little interest in religious connections or faith practice and do not value spiritual care. To them, spiritual care is a liability because it is a financial drain on the institution rather than a billable service.

A second reason that spiritual care has experienced this metamorphosis is the federal government plays a major role in health care. Regulatory and accrediting bodies require sensitive attention to spiritual needs. As the Joint Commission on the Accreditation of Healthcare Organizations (JCAHO, 1998) makes clear, "Patients have a fundamental right to considerate care that safeguards their personal dignity and respects their cultural, psychosocial, and spiritual values."[80] Because of government involvement, Medicare drives health systems. Medicare's Conditions of Participation dictate every role in health care including chaplaincy.

The institution of chaplaincy has experienced broad changes because of implementing the new directives dictated from secular and governmental sources. The form of spirituality commonly held by health care organizations has also inundated chaplain education and professional practice. It has left these structures in confusion regarding their educational model and professional methods.

EFFECT ON CHAPLAIN EDUCATION AND PRACTICE

There exists a fine line of distinction in Chaplain Education about the place of care provided to patients. Chaplains often must choose between conforming to institutional and governmental standards and their faith in Christ. This is difficult because of the contradictions within its profession. Notice the contradictions in the *Standards of the Association for Clinical Pastoral Education* (APCE).

First, chaplain education standards state what the student must do to acquire and keep certification as a professional chaplain. 1.) They must have a graduate theological education or its equivalency. 2.) They must have an endorsement by a faith group or a demonstrated connection to a recognized religious community and 3.) They must have the equivalent of one year of Clinical Pastoral Education in postgraduate training, in an accredited program recognized by the constituent organization.

---

[80]   Carey, Raymond. (1985). *Change in Perceived Need, Value and Role of Hospital Chaplains.* New York, Crossroad Publishing Company, pp. 28-41.

Chaplains must maintain good standing in their faith group as a credentialed minister. Each chaplain must hold Master of Divinity degree or its equivalent. Each must be ordained or commissioned to function in ministry by a recognized religious group as determined by ACPE. Their faith group must give them its official endorsement. Finally, students must demonstrate the ability to make effective use of their religious and spiritual heritage, theological understanding, and knowledge of the behavioral sciences in their pastoral care. In other words, Chaplain Education protocol expects its students to be Christian ministers and represent their respective denominations.

While students are required to be clergy, they must hold to other requirements that are in direct violation of their personal faith and practice as ministers. Part of their pastoral competence is to provide pastoral ministry to diverse people, taking into consideration multiple elements of cultural and ethnic differences, social conditions, and justice issues *without imposing their own perspectives*. To do so is incompatible with program standards and grounds for dismissal.

> *"Chaplains must hold to other requirements that are in direct violation of their personal faith and practice as ministers".*

Student standards require that they must not discriminate against anyone because of race, gender, age, faith group, national origin, sexual orientation, or disability. They must also approach the religious convictions of a person or group with respect and sensitivity, avoid imposing their theology or cultural values on those served. Lastly, they must maintain professional relationships with other persons in the institution in which may be employed.[81]

In looking at the standards for chaplain education, it becomes apparent that there are significant contradictions that students must come to terms with.

- Students must maintain their role as ministers while not sharing their personal faith.

---

[81] Professional Ethics Manual https://www.manula.com/manuals/acpe/acpe-manuals/2016/en/topic/new-certification-manual (Accessed November 8, 2022).

- Students must put on a façade in which they validate the patient's beliefs system despite contradicting what they themselves believe is essential to the patients spiritual well-being.
- Students must appear to support denominational doctrine and positions although it is not true.
- Students must compromise their personal integrity as a Christian and knowingly misguide patients in their care.
- Students must support a view of pastoral care that is a dictate of secular and governmental mandates.

In an examination of professional chaplaincy, one sees the same requirements that are essential components of chaplain education. According to the standards of the *Association for Professional Chaplains* (APC), the primary responsibility of the chaplain is to reach across faith group boundaries and not proselytize. Acting on behalf of their institutions, they seek to protect patients from unwelcomed forms of *spiritual intrusion.* Intrusion in this case, means that chaplains serve as a gatekeeper to keep other forms of spirituality out. Although chaplains serve as liaisons to the patient's community of faith, they invariably feel the input of other clergy into their realm is an imposition. Often, they view this care as ineffective.

Unfortunately, chaplain rules prevent them from sharing their personal values, beliefs or training. It is a wonder that Christian ministers work in health care because they cannot use their theological education in any way. Emasculating their ministry has made them ineffective. They have no other skills but to mollify the patient emotionally. Chaplains cannot pray or read scripture to a patient unless the situation is "appropriate". To maintain their good standing with the APC, they must provide an inclusive, diverse, "watered down" form of spiritual care. As such, they must provide spiritual care that respects diversity and differences including, but not limited to culture, gender, and sexual orientation and spiritual and religious practices. Many chaplains have no latitude to plan worship according to their theological understanding. Frequently, chaplains must conduct public worship services without reference to God, but instead, offer a form of worship that placates all faiths.

Because of these standards of care, chaplains focus their spirituality outside traditional religious constructs and theology. They proclaim the belief that all people share deep existential needs and concerns that are met outside conventional means. They accept that people, both inside and outside traditional religious structures, report profound spiritual experiences. These include feelings of transcendence, wonder, awe, joy, and connection to nature, and self when illness strikes. They use human pathos and a sense of altruism to help patients find meaning and preserve hope when illness strikes. Chaplains support the notion that they provide spiritual care because the questions they deal with leads to answers to existential questions such as, "Why do I exist? Why am I ill? Will I die? and What will happen to me when I die?"[82]

CHAPLAINS AND ALTERNATIVE MEDICINE

Another role the chaplain fulfills is to provide assessment for the appropriateness and coordination of complementary therapies. Patients increasingly show interest in healing from many sources not indigenous to traditional healthcare disciplines. As we have demonstrated, many complementary healing traditions ground themselves in Eastern religion. Chaplains may utilize or refer patients to complementary therapists. These include guided imagery and relaxation techniques, meditation, music therapy, and Healing Touch. This list is in no way exclusive.

Rabbi Michael J. Schorin D. Min., chaplain at the Lieberman Geriatric Health Center in Skokie, Illinois, sees the influence of alternative medicine in chaplaincy. Rabbi Schorin comments that, "I find spiritual care changing slowly, but still changing. I have brought in an *acupuncturist* to help a patient in a psych unit dealing with an over stimulated *kundalini*. I have seen *massage* and *aromatherapy* help to put people at ease. I have even used *Reiki* at times.

More importantly, I have used *visualization* to help people get to a deeper level. I was formerly a chaplain at a large tertiary hospital where the issue was getting enough time to see the patients. How many times could I see them before they left the hospital? Simply talking was too slow and not efficacious enough".

"In one small Midwest state, the three largest hospice organizations offer alternative spiritual care through their chaplain programs".

---

[82]   https://www.manula.com/manuals/acpe/acpe-manuals/2016/en/topic/
       cover-page (Accessed December 3, 2022).

Instead of being an instrument to affect Judeo-Christian care for patients, chaplains must treat patients with the occult. In one small Midwest state, the three largest hospice organizations offer alternative spiritual care through their chaplain programs. These hospice's websites advertise that their chaplains provide various alternative practices including Healing Touch, Reiki, Guided Imagery, Dream Interpretation, Visualization and Chelation Therapy. Nurses offer additional alternative therapies as well.

Because of this information, we must ask what the role of the chaplain is in health care. What does it consist of? A suggested job description for professional chaplains is available through the APC. It includes the following specifications for their chaplains:

- Grief and loss care
- Risk screening – identifying individuals whose religious and spiritual conflicts may compromise recovery or satisfactory adjustment
- Facilitation of spiritual issues related to organ and tissue donation
- Crisis intervention and Critical Incident Stress Debriefing
- Spiritual assessment
- Communication with caregivers
- Facilitation of staff communication
- Conflict resolution among staff members, patients, and family members
- Referral to internal and external resources
- Assistance with decision making and communication regarding
- decedent affairs
- Staff support relative to personal crises or work stress
- Institutional support during organizational change or crisis

From the list above, it is easy to see why the role of the chaplain is changing and in essence is spiritually bankrupt. In many ways, the role of the chaplain has more in common with social work than pastoral care. While the social worker's role is valid and important, the chaplain has no such training or expertise. He cannot practice within his area of expertise. He is under prohibitions disallowing him the ability to exercise his field of expertise in Scripture, theology and pastoral care. The institution he works for, as well as federal mandate prohibits him from practicing the theological expertise he is qualified to give. If health care organizations want to promote a secularized form of "spiritual care" they should look to people with training in the social sciences to perform spiritual care and not Christian ministers.

What can you expect from your next chaplain's visit if you are a patient in an inpatient facility? The chaplain's visit may look much like the following scenario. Your chaplain will begin their visit by providing active listening. They will want to hear your story so they may assess what your emotional and spiritual needs are. Because chaplains are naturally loving and caring people, they provide a good deal of empathy and enter your personal journey. They will help you discover meaning from your experiences of loss and grief and elicit related needs. Chaplains will also try to find how your spirituality provides an avenue to help you during your time of vulnerability and weakness. They may even act as liaison between you and your spiritual leader in the community. Prayer may be part of the visit, but only if it seems "appropriate" or is at a patient's request.

During the visit, your chaplain will gauge your spiritual tenor, measuring moment by moment what spiritual care, if any, you may be open to receiving. Depending on your mood, your chaplain may discuss your mutual love of fishing, or your family's last get together instead of a having a spiritual conversation. Chaplains are master chameleons; able to subtlety shift their approach to whatever situation confronts them. One patient made the comment in disgust that his chaplain was "the master of a thousand disguises".

CONSIDERATIONS FOR CHAPLAINS

Pastoral care is of paramount concern at anytime, but especially during the vulnerable moments associated with hospitalization. For most patients, it is a time in their lives when they are facing a crisis. They may even be facing the final crisis in life as they prepare to leave this existence for eternity. Most people have questions they need answered. They want to know the truth and have assurance that they are ready to meet Christ. Even nominal Christians want a sense of peace knowing that they are going to heaven.

The chaplain's role is vital at this juncture in people's lives. Since 42% of patients have no church affiliation because of varying circumstances, the chaplain may be the only spiritual figure they encounter during their illness or impending death. With this in mind, it is imperative the

Christian chaplain does just that, acts as a Christian. The seriousness of the situation demands it!

"42% of patients have no church affiliation; the chaplain may be the only spiritual figure they encounter during their illness or impending death".

The considerations below are for chaplains, but they equally true for any Christian who works in the health care industry. In addition, Christians who volunteer in health care will find these considerations worth studying too. All believers may eventually become an inpatient and should consider them too. As you read these statements, let the weight of their implications cause you to consider your response to the questions they ask.

1. There is a lack of clarity and consistency about what the term 'spirituality' means. We have looked at some definitions of the term and the implications for chaplains delivering spiritual care. We have thought about the challenges faced by a chaplain who has a personal faith in Christ and who wishes to give authentic Christian care.

2. The emerging concept of spirituality as having a relationship with a higher being, raises discussion about the relationship between spirituality and religion. We must answer the question whether the two can actually be separated or whether "spirituality" as defined in health care is a cult-like phenomenon

3. A key ingredient in this definition is separating spirituality from religion and God so spirituality can aspire to having universal appeal. The highest goal in defining spirituality, is not to achieve accuracy or find truth, but to be inclusive.

4. The problem exists because the definition places spirituality outside God, and outside of Christ. Potential difficulty over this distinction arises for the chaplain when discerning and meeting a patient's spiritual need. It becomes important when the question asks, whether a person can be spiritually healthy, or whole, without

God. If a chaplain's aim is to aid a patient's restoration to full spiritual health, it becomes of fundamental importance whether God is needed for this end.

5. Are chaplains spiritual shape-shifters, prohibited from sharing their personal beliefs except when specifically asked. The difficulty is inescapable. How can chaplains, operating under one belief system, Christianity, offer spiritual care to patients who hold opposing views?

6. As Christians, we know that a person's wholeness, their physical, emotional, social and spiritual integration can only become a reality through a dynamic and personal relationship with Christ. Florence Nightingale regarded nursing as concerned with the body as a temple of the Spirit of God. From a Christian perspective, we assert the reason that people need God is because they are incomplete without Him. God created them to be in relationship with Him. The sole purpose of human life is that, *'In Him we live and move and have our being'* (Acts 17:28). Jesus Christ claimed to be the Bread of Life and described man's relationship with him using an analogy of branches stemming from a vine (John15). If it is true that only God can meet a person's spiritual needs through a relationship with Jesus Christ, this has enormous implications for the chaplain who knows Him.

7. A tension exists between professionalism and spirituality in Chaplaincy. Chaplain programs show that in an attempt to become more professional, the chaplain's role has made a deliberate move away from its spiritual heritage.

8. There is great frustration in the practice of chaplaincy. Chaplains must provide spiritual care in an atmosphere where spiritual needs go unrecognized. Chaplains cannot address authentic spiritual issues, but are required to leave patients without a spiritual cure.

9.   Christian chaplains are responsible for caring for the spiritual needs of their patients as well as those of their family and friends. Many of them find themselves torn in two directions. On the one hand, they may feel bound to do all in their power to bring those in their care into a relationship with God, through Christ. While on the other hand they may feel that this approach is not acceptable by colleagues or employers. Chaplain's like this face accusations of failing to be non-judgmental in their care and abusing their position. It may even cost them their job as they faithfully represent Christ.

10.   The chaplain is accountable to their profession that may be ambivalent in its stance on spiritual care giving. This environment may even be hostile to the sharing of their faith. However, the chaplain who lives under the authority of Jesus has a higher calling. Jesus' final commission to his followers was to *"make disciples of all nations"* (Matthew, 28:19).

11.   The present-day model of spiritual care fails to recognize the Christian chaplain longs to share the source of freedom and wholeness in Christ with the patients and families they serve.

12.   The Christian chaplain clearly cannot be responsible for a patient's everlasting salvation. It is only the chaplain's duty to present the patient with as much of the truth as they understand and find suitable circumstances to share their faith. Chaplains must respect the patient's response. Ultimately, patients' spiritual well-being is their own responsibility.

SUMMARY AND CONCLUSIONS

The role of the chaplain is hopelessly contorted, confused and inconsistent. This is not only true in the chaplain's daily work place, but is also part of the fabric of chaplain education and professional accrediting bodies. In many respects, the chaplain is not even sure of what their role is. They must constantly be on guard that they are not imposing their own views on patients. Chaplains must maintain a strict non-judgmental view. This means that their concern is not the spiritual well-being of their patient, but the institution's policy. If a chaplain fails to do this, it may cost them their job.

> *"This means that their concern is not the spiritual well-being of their patient, but the institution's policy".*

"Pastoral care" has transformed itself into "spiritual care", with different shades of meaning than traditional Christianity. Religion has divorced itself from spirituality in the health care setting. Chaplains cannot use their theological education, training and experience to provide care as Christian ministers. Instead, secular health care institutions and governmental agencies mandate the means of spiritual care.

If the chaplain tries to share that which he is qualified in, his Christian faith, he is failing to provide non-judgmental care and imposing his religious viewpoint on his patients. In many respects, the healthcare chaplain operates in the sphere of social work or as a psychotherapist, areas in which he has no training or qualification.

Worst of all, health care chaplains must violate their own personal faith. They must betray their own integrity, they must compromise their faith in Christ and they must mislead and misguide those who are spiritually vulnerable. Whether passively or purposely, they are guilty of ignoring what they know as the truth and directing their patients away from Christ. Unfortunately, some health care chaplains have sacrificed themselves on the altar of financial security. It is unavoidable if they want a job. Another truth is that scores of chaplains from liberal denominations believe in Universalism. Universalism is the idea that everyone spends eternity in heaven. To them, matters of faith in Christ and a personal relationship with Him may be a moot issues.

Most chaplains are good and loving people. They provide genuine compassion and care. They possess skills that will provide you a kind of solace and respite in your illness. However, for all their good intentions, chaplains are powerless to provide care as representatives of Christ. They are aware of the system and philosophy that they work in, but will still provide the best care they can. Nevertheless, if they are a person of genuine faith in Christ, it will nag at them, and they will feel torn by a sense of inner consternation. They may not identify it right away, but they are experiencing the guilt that comes from compromising their faith in Christ.

Chaplains need to be careful, because they are responsible for what they do. If we are God's children, then it is not aberrant to use this passage of scripture. Jesus warned *"But if anyone causes one of these little ones who believe in me to sin, it would be better for him to have a large millstone hung around his neck and to be drowned in the depths of the sea"* (Matthew 18:6).

STUDY QUESTIONS

THE CULT CALLED SPIRITUAL CARE

1. What is a chaplain? Why are they called "spiritual chameleons"?

2. How are "religion" and "spirituality" distinguished?

3. How is pastoral care changing? How its Christian message changed?

4. Why has Spiritual care changed?

5. What contradictions must student chaplains come to terms with in order to continue their education and practice? Why would this be difficult?

6. In what ways are chaplains asked to minimize their education, deny their faith and contradict personal integrity?

7. How does the chaplain's job resemble that of a social worker?

8. How do you envision a visit from this kind of chaplain?

9. What 12 statements are made for Chaplains to consider?

10. What special responsibility as ministers do chaplains bear according to Matthew 18:6?

CHAPTER 11
BIBLICAL PERSPECTIVES ON THE CHANGING FACE OF SPIRITUALITY IN MEDICINE

CHAPTER 11
BIBLICAL PERSPECTIVES ON THE CHANGING FACE OF SPIRITUALITY IN MEDICINE

"Children say that people are hung sometimes for speaking the truth.

— Joan of Arc

God is our healer. Healing is not only an attribute of God, but it is His Name and the way in which He identifies Himself. He is *Jehovah Rapha,* the Lord Our Healer. The New Testament reveals that Christ's atonement purchased our healing. 1 Peter 2:24 states, *"By his stripes we are healed."* That is why it is appalling when Reiki, Healing Touch and Therapeutic Touch attempt to usurp God' role as Healer and offer an "end run" around His provision for our care. Touch Therapies are a cheat. They promise wholeness but offer only spiritual brokenness and death. They are deceptive; worming their way into people's hearts and lives making them think there is an alternative to trusting God with our illnesses.

The Bible contains many accounts of healing. According to Scripture, God is the source of healing. Even conventional medicine is the gift of God. We are grateful for the care we receive from doctors and nurses, and the availability of drug therapy and surgical procedures. However, they are not an end in themselves. God designed the method and means of healing. Every drug exists because of the unique properties of plants and minerals that God created. Every surgical procedure exists because of the marvelous way God designed human anatomy.

Ultimately, medical knowledge is the gift of God and is directly attributable to Him. All attempts to find healing by alternative methods is to deny God's provision and a failure of our need to trust Him with our health. To circumvent God in the healing process is to reject our Creator. When we turn to alternatives outside the divine venue for healing, we turn to alternatives that are under the control of *"the god of this age"* (2 Corinthians 4:4). Since healing is part of God' plan and He is its only legitimate source, it is important that we have a biblical understanding of healing.

HEALING IN THE OLD TESTAMENT

God gave Israel a Healing Covenant shortly after their miraculous escape from Egypt and the crossing of the Red Sea. As they began those long years of journeying and wandering on their way to the Promised Land, we read:

> *"There he made for them a statute and an ordinance, and there he proved them, and he said, If thou wilt diligently hearken unto the voice of the Lord thy God, and wilt do that which is right in his sight, and wilt give ear to his commandments, and keep all his statutes, I will put none of these diseases upon thee, which I have brought upon the Egyptians: for I am the Lord that healeth thee"* (Ex 15:25,26).

This verse introduces the fact that healing is part of God's nature. Healing is who He is. The English transliteration of the Hebrew phrase, *"I am the Lord that healeth thee"* is *Jehovah Rapha* – the Lord our Healer. These verses record the promise of God's healing power for His people. God's nature has never changed; He is immutable. Therefore, God's power to heal is as available today as it was to the Israelites long ago. *"I am the Lord, I change not"* (Malachi 3:6).

HEALING IN THE NEW TESTAMENT

A central aspect of the Atonement of Christ is the promise of healing. The availability of healing for believers is possible through His work on the Cross. It is because of His sacrifice that we can experience God's healing power. Isaiah's prediction of the coming of the messianic Man of Sorrow's clearly portrays the correlation between healing and the atonement of

Christ. In Isaiah 53:5 God's Word records, " *But he was wounded for our transgressions, he was bruised for our iniquities: the chastisement of our peace was upon him; and with his stripes we are healed".*

"In Greek, sozo means wholeness and healing, as well as salvation".

1,500 years later, the apostle Peter unmistakably applies the atoning work of Jesus Christ as the source of God's healing power. Peter wrote, *"Who his own self bare our sins in his own body on the tree, that we, being dead to sins, should live unto righteousness: by whose stripes you were healed"* (1 Peter 2:24).

Not only is, healing part of the atonement, it is directly related to the doctrine of the *Redemption of our Bodies.* The Greek word for healing is *sozo.* Just as our dictionaries attribute several meanings to a single word, Greek lexicons do this same thing. In Greek, sozo means wholeness and healing, as well as salvation. The best application of the word *sozo* in relation to illness is that the work of salvation includes wholeness and healing.

The Greek verb associated with sozo is used in the future perfect tense. In other words sozo refers to what we have now, but is not yet complete. For example, I may borrow money and buy a car, but it is not mine free and clear until I pay off the loan. In a theological sense, healing is ours in this present age, but we anticipate its fullness in the age to come.[83]

In this present age, the act of healing announces that the New Age is here in part, but one day it will come in its totality when Christ returns. The resurrection is God's promise to believers; we will receive a new and glorified body. This is the Biblical teaching of the Redemption of the Body. The Bible declares that, *"even we ourselves groan within ourselves, waiting for the adoption, to wit, the redemption of our body"* (Rom 8:23). The body of a Christian belongs to God because he purchased it. *"What? know ye not that your body is the temple of the Holy Spirit which is in you, and ye are not your own? For ye are bought with a price?"* (1 Corinthians 6:19, 20).

Many Christians, who would never question God's claim upon the human spirit, have doubts about His desire for their health. According to Scripture, God is interested in you body, soul, and spirit. This is what the Doctrine of the Redemption of the Body affirms. Healing, wholeness and resurrection are ours in Christ. The gift of healing is ours in part, but we look forward to the Redemption of our Bodies when we will have it in its fullness.

---

[83] Wuest, Kenneth. 1973. *Wuest's Word Studies From the New Testament.* Wm. B. Eerdman's Publishing Company, Grand Rapids, Michigan.

THE MINISTRY OF HEALING IN THE CHURCH

History shows that healing by the direct power of God continued through the entire Church Age to the present time. Note the testimonies of some of the Church Fathers:

165 A.D. More than sixty-five years after the death of John, the last of the Apostles Justin Martyr writes. "There are numerous demoniacs that exist in the whole world; many of them in your own city. Some of our Christian men, exorcising them, cast them out in the name of Jesus Christ, who was crucified under Pontius Pilate. They have healed, and do heal, rendering the helpless and driving the possessing devils out of men. This happens although they could not be cured by all the other exorcists, and those who used incantations and drugs."

Writing in 192 A.D., Irenaeus declares, "Those who are in truth and receive grace from Him do in His name, perform miracles and promote the welfare of others, according to the gift, that each has received from him. Others heal the sick by laying their hands upon them, and they are whole. Yea moreover, as I have said, the dead even have been raised up, and remained among us for years."

Writing in 216 A.D., Tertullian records: "For the clerk of one of them who was liable to be thrown upon the ground by an evil spirit was set free from his affliction, as was also the relative of another, and the little boy of a third. And how many men of rank, to say nothing of the common people have been delivered from devils and healed of diseases."

Writing in 429 A.D., Theodore of Mopsuesta declares, "Many heathen amongst us are being healed by Christians from whatever sickness they have, so abundant are miracles in our midst."

In 500 A.D., Gregory the Great, believed to be the first Pope, gave away his inherited fortune, and became a missionary to Britain, praying for the people and anointing them with oil in the name of the Lord, quoting James 5:14,15.

Count Zinzendorf, a Bishop of the Moravian movement, (United Brethren), was a close friend of John Wesley. He was a deeply sincere man with a burden for World Evangelization. In writing to the Church, he states "To believe against hope is the root of the gift of miracles, and I owe this testimony to our Beloved Church, that Apostolic powers are there manifested. We have undeniable proofs thereof. In the healing of maladies in themselves incurable, such as Cancer and Consumption, and when the patient was in the agonies of death, all by means of a prayer or the word."

John Wesley wrote in his journal the following accounts about healing. "On March 19, 1741, Judith Williams, who was in grievous pain of both body and mind, after a short time of prayer, we left her. But her pain was gone, her body so strengthened that she immediately rose, and the next day went abroad." (Vol. II, 437).[84]

The gift of healing has always been available to God's people. He disclosed this through the revelation of His nature in the Old Testament, through Christ's Atonement on the Cross, and through the work of the Holy Spirit in the Church. We have every expectation that God's healing power remains available today.

THE GIFT OF THE LAYING ON OF HANDS

Scripture talks a great deal about using human hands to enact spiritual realities. The first place we read about the laying on of hands in Genesis 48:14 where Jacob lays his hands on the heads of Josephs sons, Manasseh and Ephraim. In this, he was acting as the paternal and spiritual head of his family to extend the patriarchal blessing to the next generation.

We see the laying on of hands again in Numbers 27:18-23 and Deuteronomy 34:9. Here, both Moses and Joshua lay their hands on Aaron, his sons and the Levites to *consecrate* them before the Lord. Another important scripture that portrays the laying on of hands is Leviticus 14:21. In this verse, the Bible states that the high priest transferred *guilt* to the Scape Goat on the Great Day of Atonement by means of the laying on of hands.

Although there are many instances of God's healing in the Old Testament, 2 Kings 4:34 clearly records an act of healing by laying on of hands through the prophet Elisha. The Bible states that the prophet Elisha placed his hands upon the hands of a child and through his touch, God healed the boy.

"There can no doubt that the gift of laying on of hands is a cardinal doctrine of the Church".

---

[84]   Duffield, Guy and Van Cleave, Nathaniel. 1983. *Foundations of Pentecostal Theology*. L.I.F.E. Bible College, Los Angeles, CA. pp. 536, 537.

The New Testament records the continuance of God's gift of laying on of hands to work in His people's lives. Matthew 19:15 observes that Jesus laid his hands upon the small children that came to Him and blessed them.

In Acts 9:17 we see Saul, blinded by the appearance of Jesus on the Damascus Road. The Bible records that Ananias "put his hands on him" healing him and imparting the gift of the Holy Spirit. 1 Corinthians 12:1-11 records that the laying on of hands is to bestow the gifts of the Spirit.

Finally, laying on of hands appears in the commissioning of Paul and Barnabas in Acts 13:33 and in the ordination of Timothy in 1 Timothy 4:14. *There can no doubt that the gift of laying on of hands is a cardinal doctrine of the Church.* Nearly every denomination today uses this gift in some manner in its services.

In the context of touch therapies, it is important to note that one of the reasons that God has ordained the gift of the laying on of hands *is to heal the sick.* Jesus declares this in Mark 16:17,18, *"These signs shall follow them that believe. In my name they shall lay hands on the sick, and they shall recover."* Notice that there is no mention of anointing with oil, or of praying for the sick. All that it says is that those who believe shall lay their hands on the sick in the name of Jesus. Jesus used this method on a number of occasions. In the following scriptures, Jesus touched the sick, or laid His hand or hands upon them: Matt 8:15; Mark 6:5; 8:23, 25; Luke 4:40; 5:13; 13:13. Today, when believers lay hands on the sick in the name of Jesus, it is as though the hands of Jesus extend through them.

We need to be careful that we are not quick to lay hands on other people, or have others lay hands on us. 1 Timothy 5:22 tells us, *"Lay hands suddenly on no man, neither be partaker of other men's sins: keep thyself pure".* If Scripture instructs us to be careful in laying hands on others, we should also be even more careful whom we allow to lay hands on us. Practitioners of touch therapies often mislead the sick by offering to "pray for them". They will tell them that they are acting as an extension of the ministry of Jesus. Some will even come in the name of a church. However, beware of what Jesus said, *"false prophets, will come to you in sheep's clothing, but inwardly they are ravening wolves"* (Matthew 7:15).

COUNTERFEITS OF GOD'S GIFT

We have gone to great lengths to show the Biblical basis of healing, and its continued use throughout the history of the Church. We have also been diligent to describe the gift of the laying on of hands. We know that God has ordained laying on of hands as a gift to offer us the reality of healing. God does not offer an empty promise, nor does He offer cheap imitations. God has compassion for his children that suffer from illnesses of every kind and offers the reality of His healing power through Christ Jesus. He gives this gift to us through the Person of the Holy Spirit by the laying on of hands of fellow believers. God offers the real thing. Is it any wonder that Satan would attempt to counterfeit this precious gift by scheming, deceiving and implementing touch therapies?

We must understand that Reiki only imitates the gift of God. Therapeutic Touch attempts to impersonate the reality of the healing power of the Holy Spirit. Healing Touch mimics the scriptural injunction to lay hands on the sick so they may recover. Each touch therapy is an act of deception. The Bible states that those who teach these practices *"belong to their father, the devil, and they want to carry out their father's desire. He was a murderer from the beginning, not holding to the truth, for there is no truth in him. When he speaks a lie, he speaks of his own for he is a liar and the father of it"*.

"Exposing a lie to the light of God's Word defeats it like a moth drawn to a flame."

How should Christians deal with a counterfeit? As a bank teller holds a false bill to the light to see its discrepancies, our job is to expose spiritual counterfeits to the light of Christ. We must expose them with the truth. In John 17:17 Jesus prays, *"Sanctify them through thy truth: thy word is truth"*. We must expose them by teaching the truth of God's Word and we must expose them by preaching the truth of God's Word. Exposing a lie to the light of God's Word defeats it like a moth drawn to a flame.

THE DANGERS OF REIKI

Reiki is an offshoot of Buddhism. It is not an alternative medicine; it is a belief and a practice. Dr. Mikao Usui taught as a college professor at a Christian school, was a graduate of a prestigious seminary in the United States, but abandoned his faith in Christ for Buddhism. His method of healing came to him in a vision. This was not a God-given vision, but one that came out of the practice of Buddhist asceticism. He tinkered in contacting spirits guides, deceased ancestors and animal spirits.

Reiki derives its concept of a Universal Life Force from the Buddhist concept of pantheism that "god is all and all is god". This spiritual construct believes that the divine manifests itself as a universal force of energy composed of all living things permeating the air we breathe. Without any medical or scientific evidence, Reiki practitioners believe in the existence of energy vortexes of the *chakra* system. Supposedly, the practitioner *channels* energy into these vortexes. From there, it flows into the *marma* points and travels along the *meridian* lines to the diseased organ that needs healed. These beliefs are so much rubbish because there is no way to substantiate any of them.

Reiki practitioners go through three rites of initiation called degrees. A Reiki Master confers these degrees upon initiates. He uses the secret symbols of Reiki to channel spiritual energy into the student. Initiation rites are occultic because they introduce the student to spirit guides, practice necromancy and animism. While not admitting it, the Reiki Master acts as a medium by contacting a familiar spirit that remains with the student for life. This spirit gives guidance, answers questions and assists in the healing process. Recipients of Reki must be careful, for Reiki opens doors to the spirit world dominated by the forces of Satan. Scripture warns us, "*do not give the devil a foothold*" (Ephesians 4:27).

THE THREAT OF THERAPEUTIC TOUCH

Therapeutic Touch is spiritually dangerous. Its co-founder, Dora Kunz, held the dual position as president of the Theosophical Society and editor-in-chief of the Theosophical Publishing House. She was a committed cultist. Not only was she a cultist, she was also a dedicated Spiritist, dabbling in the dark arts of the occult.

As a theosophist, she was well-versed in syncretism or the mixing of religious ideas and practices. As evidenced from her writings, she was just as apt to quote from Buddhist inscriptions, books on Theosophy, and the Bible all in the same breath. She was a master of deceit. The purpose of syncretism is always to create confusion. Its goal is to seduce its listeners into believing a lie. As with any cult, Theosophy is most effective when dealing with nominal Christians who are minimally familiar with God's

Word. Luke-warm Christians are also easily led astray. It is no wonder that the apostle Paul admonishes believers to, *"study to show thyself approved unto God, a workman that need not to be ashamed, rightly dividing the word of truth* (2 Timothy 2:15).

As a Spiritist, Kunz claimed that she was the fourteenth generation in her family able to see etheric (auras) bodies. She used this gift to discover where client's etheric bodies were out of balance and in need of healing. Kunz admits in her books that she has the gifts of clairvoyance and clairaudience. Through the practice of centering, assessment and intervention, she states that she contacts spirits, allowing them to channel through her and connect with the client. It would be fair to state that Kunz's therapy is not an alternative form of medicine, but is the work of a charlatan.

The other co-founder of Therapeutic Touch is Delores Krieger. She continues to live at the Theosophical Retreat Center in Pumpkin Hollow in Careyville, New York. Krieger takes a somewhat different approach to Therapeutic Touch. She suggests a scientific methodology behind her work in an effort to garner credibility. She attempts to use physics, field theory, electromagnetic fields and electricity to explain how Therapeutic Touch works. She expanded the theories of corresponding fields and proposed the existence of bio-energy and psychogenic fields.

Eventually, she leaves her scientific latticework behind and moves into the realm of the occult. Krieger uses her presuppositions to introduce the idea of communicating with spirits and other higher life forms through psychogenic fields. She uses the idea of a human bio-field to discuss how the body channels *prana* or Vital Life Energy. This part of her theory is directly dependent on Hindu philosophy and religion. She hypothesizes that healing occurs by channeling *prana* into the *chakra system, marma points and meridian lines.* Krieger offers no evidence that these systems exist, but simply presupposes that they do.

According to Krieger, Therapeutic Touch therapists *center* themselves in preparation for treatments much as a medium enters a trance. During *assessment,* they contact *spirit guides* for guidance and information. *Intervention* includes using *clairsentience* to feel cold and hot spots and ascertain electromagnetic fields along the *marma* points. It is at these points that energy becomes the foci.

Krieger is also a strong proponent of communication with *inanimate objects*. She claims to receive supernatural information from inanimate objects as evidenced in her stories. Likewise, Krieger admits to using Spiritism and shamanism in her practice of Therapeutic Touch. Although she does a masterful job of wrapping Therapeutic Touch in scientific jargon, she just as readily admits that her therapy is a variant of Hindu religious practices.

As a Theosophist, Krieger is an expert at blending other faiths with Christianity. This is dangerous because it appeals to immature or nominal Christians that are less familiar with God's Word. 1 Peter 5:8 warns, *"Be sober, be vigilant; because your adversary the devil, as a roaring lion, walks about, seeking whom he may devour"*.

THE PERILS OF HEALING TOUCH

Janet Mentger developed Healing Touch in 1985 and supported her work by building the Colorado Healing Touch Center. Mentger studied the work of Kunz and Krieger. However, she felt that there must be more emphasis on systematizing the method and providing a model of education.

Like Krieger, Janet Mentger went to great lengths to develop a pseudoscientific explanation of Healing Touch to give her theory credibility. Healing Touch revolves around the idea that there is an electro-magnetic field that exists throughout nature and even into space itself. All living things are subject to this field and interact with it. Mentger hypothesized that normal electric flow goes through the hands of the therapist and into the human body.

Eventually, Mentger deviated from a strictly scientific model, interweaving it with a spiritually based system of thought. Mentger was aware of the teaching of Theosophy through her association with Kunz and Krieger. She was also familiar with their Eastern religious views. Added to this, the writings of Barbara Brennan also influenced her thought development. She paid particular attention to Brennan's study of the human aura. Along with this, Mentger gave herself to the study of Theosophy, Hinduism and Spiritism. She synthesized ideas from each of these religious viewpoints to develop Healing Touch. Many people find these influences confusing, but to a Theosophist, Healing Touch makes perfect sense.

"Over 80,000 nurses have been trained as Healing Touch therapists".

One of Mentger's primary concerns was to make Healing Touch palatable to the medical world. Her chief way of doing this was to develop an educational model that ended in certification and licensing. She developed a five-year curriculum and an international licensing board to fulfill this aspect of her mission. This model has proven most effective in appealing to the medical world. At this time, over 80,000 nurses have been trained as Healing Touch therapists and it is part of the curriculum at 80 medical schools. Required class reading features the writings of Annie Besant, Helena Blavatsky, Charles Leadbeater, Alice Bailey, Barbara Brennan, Deepak Chopra and Larry Dossey M.D. to name a few New Age personalities.

The spiritual problems associated with Healing Touch are obvious to Christians when they read the list of required courses. Classes are available in aura reading, mind clearing, the development of higher sense perception and developing other psychic abilities. In its course description of a class on higher sense perception the catalog states, *"Make no mistake…intuition, clairvoyance, telepathy, and yes being psychic—these are all part of Higher Sense Perception. You will see a natural increase of these abilities with this course. However, you will also experience how life is really supposed to feel here on Earth. A life full of joy, empowerment and filled* with *a sense of purpose in a multidimensional world—that is Higher Sense Perception Living".* Instructors advise students that during this class they should expect to meet their spirit guide or angel who will assist them in their work.

Two things make Healing Touch particularly dangerous. First, is its ability to convince the medical establishment that it is a relevant medical modality. As we have seen earlier, there is no evidence to support this. Second, Healing Touch is expert at cloaking itself in Christian terminology to make it palpable to those in the Church. Many churches and chaplaincy programs offer courses in Healing Touch.

This is substantiated through the words of Healing Touch advocate Dorothea Hover-Kramer. She writes, "The Spiritual Ministry Program is now an affiliate of the Colorado Center for Healing Touch, standing on its own as an interpretation of energy healing concepts in Judeo-Christian language. Linda Smith, founder, writes, 'the program was born 3 1/2 years ago to answer the unique needs of those who wish to learn hands-on healing for church and spiritual ministry settings'. The program appeals especially to parish nurses and nurses wishing to understand the laying on of hands and other Healing Touch techniques. The program also appeals to ministers from all denominations as well as chaplains. The lay community also seeks to explore the spiritual healing ministry. The aim of the program is to help bring healing back into our faith communities and ministry and service settings everywhere".[85]

Proponents of Healing Touch are not trying to bring the ministry of healing back into the church. Instead, they are attempting to deceive the church into believing that Healing Touch is an extension of the ministry of Jesus. The truth is that Healing Touch thrives on the "doctrines of demons". 1 Timothy 4:1 admonishes us, *"Now the Spirit speaks expressly, that in the latter times some shall depart from the faith, giving heed to seducing spirits, and doctrines of devils".*

WHERE DO TOUCH THERAPIES GO WRONG?

Cults and the occult have one feature in common. They deny the basic ingredients of the Christian faith. They blatantly attack and minimize the most fundamental doctrines of Scripture. Examining this commonality will help us identify the corrupt nature of touch therapies.

Denial of A Personal God — Touch therapies go wrong because they deny the essence of the gospel. The injunction to refute non-Christian concepts concerning God and the Lord Jesus Christ are explicit in Scripture. The personality of God and the deity of Christ are indispensable to Christianity along with other essentials of faith that touch therapists deny. The God of the Bible created man and is separate and distinct from him (Gen 1:27). He is a cognizant ego or personality (Ex 3:14; Isa 48:12; John 8:58), and He is triune -- three separate persons -- Father, Son, and Holy Spirit, yet one in essence or nature (Deut 6:4; Gal 3:20). The laws of language, logic, and biblical theology can permit nothing else.

Denial of Redemption through Christ — Reiki, Healing Touch and Therapeutic Touch want no part of the vicarious sacrifice of Jesus. In fact,

---

[85]   Hover-Kramer, Dorethea. 2002. *Healing Touch: A Guidebook for Practitioners.* Albany, New York: Delmar: Thompson Learning. p. 150.

Christ's death is personally repugnant to them. By their own admission, they say that it is "an ignoble belief" to think that we can fling our sins upon another. Nevertheless, this is exactly what Scripture calls us to do throughout the New Testament.

The Bible bears incontrovertible witness to the truth that *"Christ died for the ungodly"* (Rom 5:6), and that *"The blood of Jesus Christ... cleanses us from all sin"* (1 John 1:7). There is no doctrine substantiated within the pages of the Bible better than that of the substitutionary death of Christ for the sins of the world.

Denial of the Power of Prayer — The biblical doctrine of prayer also suffers at the hand of touch therapies. In the biblical vocabulary, prayer is communion with a personal God, not an abstract force or a cosmic consciousness. Jesus Christ himself encouraged us to pray many times (see Matt 5:44; 6:6-7, 9; 9:38). He repeatedly emphasized its virtues and benefits. For the Christian, prayer is the link with the Eternal by which we can come to *"the throne of grace"* in the power of the Holy Spirit and find *"grace to help in time of need"* (Heb 4:16).

Denial of Judgment for Sin — The Bible plainly states that all men have come under the divine indictment of sin (Rom 3:23). The only remedy for sin is the redemptive work of Jesus Christ who *"died, the just for the unjust to bring us to God"* (1 Peter 3:18). There can be little doubt that touch therapists, consider that salvation exists through karma and reincarnation. There is no God of love. Their god takes the penalty of sin and tries to deal with it on the wheel of reincarnation and infinite progression. Salvation for the Christian is by grace and faith in God's method for making men holy and through the only *"name under heaven given among men, whereby we must be saved"* (Acts 4:12).

Denial of Sin, Salvation and Hell — Contrasted to the biblical picture of sin and salvation, touch therapies equate God the Father with the pagan gods Buddha and Brahma. Touch therapists believe that appeasing the wrath of a righteous God for sin is by suffering in *Kamaloka*, "the temporal place of suffering". To them personal salvation is obtained through various reincarnations ending in the absorption of the individual. These ideas cannot be reconciled with biblical revelation, but they are all that the touch therapist has to offer.

THE REALM OF THE OCCULT

When we study alternative medicine and the therapies of Reki, Therapeutic, Touch and Healing Touch, we discover that we have entered into the realm of the occult. When studying the occult, we enter into the kingdom of the Evil One, Satan.

For the Christian, Hinduism and its worship of 330 million gods and goddesses is nothing more than the worship of demons. The apostle Paul describes their power structure in Ephesians 6:12 where he writes, *"For we wrestle not against flesh and blood, but against principalities, against powers, against the rulers of the darkness of this world, against spiritual wickedness in high places"*.

Buddhism's belief system that mixes an ethical construct with ancestor and spirit worship is an abomination before the Lord. Theosophy's syncretistic mishmash denies that Jesus is *"The Way the Truth and the Life"* (John 14:6). Spiritism's focus on life after death delves into the black arts where Satan and his demons dwell. The founders of each of the touch therapies brazenly admit to the exercise of these occult practices. How can anyone think these are simply benign therapies with no religious correlation after reading these words? We do not lie when we say that the occult is penetrating health care as never before and thousands are blind to it. This book is an attempt to open the eyes of the Church, Christians and health care workers to the spiritual dangers that are entering our medical organizations.

THE PRINCE AND POWER OF THE AIR

If there is one verse that every Christian should be aware of in the context of Touch Therapies and alternative medicine, it is Ephesians 2:1-2. Here the apostle Paul writes, *"And you hath he quickened, who were dead in trespasses and sins; Wherein in time past ye walked according to the course of this world, according to the prince and the power of the air, the spirit that now works in the children of disobedience"*. It is imperative that we understand the depths of the Satanic in the touch therapies we have discussed.

The one element that all three touch therapies have in common is the pantheistic belief in the Universal Life Energy. This force consists of all things, surrounds all things, and permeates all things. The pantheistic idea that "all is god and god is all" is the driving force behind Reiki, Therapeutic Touch and Healing Touch. According to practitioners, the Universal Life Force infuses the air that surrounds us.

In Ephesians 2:1-2, the Bible, says that Satan is *"the prince and power of the air".* The Greek language used in this verse indicates that Satan inhabits the "lower atmosphere." The air around us is the realm of his power and influence. It is also the realm is which each of us lives and in which Satan attempts to attack us. Our conclusion: the alternative therapies of Reiki, Healing Touch, and Therapeutic Touch are empowered by no one less than the Devil himself. The Energy that touch therapists draw upon is in fact, Satanic power. These are strong words, but we must fully expose the Satanic practices of touch therapies to the glorious light of the Gospel of Christ in order to reveal their incredible darkness. The apostle John wrote, *"God is light, and in him is no darkness at all"* (1 John 1:5).

The challenge is that many people are blind to the truth and are deceived. Unfortunately, some Christian medical personnel are aware of these therapies yet, have no idea about the spiritual dimension that lies behind them. Some Christians while hospitalized have had nurses offer them alternative treatments and accepted them glibly unaware of what they were. Unfortunately, there are Christians who have been trained in touch therapies and are shocked to learn what they have participated in. Remember, Satan's number one job is to deceive. In 2 Corinthians 4: 3-5 the apostle Paul reveals this. He writes, *"and even if our gospel is veiled, it is veiled to those who are perishing. The god of this age has blinded the minds of unbelievers, so that they cannot see the light of the gospel of the glory of Christ, who is the image of God".*

> **"When we study alternative medicine a we discover that we have entered into the realm of the occult".**

Nurse and doctors, pastors and Christians, must wake up to what is happening in our hospitals and hospices. As an individual, you may not have encountered touch therapies yet, but you will. The occult is rapidly penetrating our health care system. Chaplains are impotent and a new trend has emerged conveniently called "spiritual care". Paul warns us in Ephesians 6:10, *"Finally, my brethren, be strong in the Lord, and in the power of his might. Put on the whole armor of God that ye may be able to stand against the wiles of the devil."*

It is important to recognize that some readers of this book are aware of the alternative therapies written about here. Other individuals may have received training to perform them and unknowingly delved into the realm of the occult. Because of their work environments or subtle pressure by their supervisors, some Christian nurses have received training in touch therapies. Out of sheer ignorance, some in the Church have thought that touch therapies are an extension of Jesus' healing ministry. Even chaplains have been deceived and have received training in touch therapies. Of course, it is quite possible that as a patient, you too have encountered alternative medicine. These therapies may seem benign at first, nevertheless, the Bible admonishes us to *"Abstain from all appearance of evil"* (1 Thessalonians 5:2).

For those who feel a sense of remorse, a sense of guilt or condemnation for their involvement with touch therapies, we must turn to the grace that is available in the Word of God. The Bible reminds us, *"For if our heart condemns us, God is greater than our heart, and knows all things"* (1John 3:20). Romans 8:1 repeats this same promise, *"There is therefore now no condemnation to them which are in Christ Jesus".*

We must recognize that some Christians have become aware of the dangers of touch therapies for the first time and feel a sense of fear regarding them. You may ask yourself, "What have I gotten into"? For the believer, Scripture announces freedom from fear and is the fountainhead of the peace only God can offer. Jesus assures us *"If the Son therefore shall make you free, ye shall be free indeed"* (John 8:36). 1 John 4:4 reminds us that *"greater is he that is in you, than he that is in the world".*

AN OPPORTUNITY TO MEET CHRIST

In view of the reality of the occult, knowing Jesus Christ is all-important. If you have been reading this book and realize that you do not know Jesus as your personal Savior, perhaps you would like to make that decision today. To accept Christ is not a difficult thing, but you must simply mean it with all of your heart.

First, the Bible tells us in Romans 3:10, *"There is none righteous, no not one."* The first step to knowing Christ is to repent. This means that with God's help, we commit to a 180-degree turn around from the sin in our lives. Second, the Bible says that we need to ask for God's forgiveness for our sin. Romans 6:23 states that, *"The wages of sin is death"*. The penalty for sin is eternity without God. That is the bad news. The good news is part of that very same verse. *"But the gift of God is eternal life through Jesus Christ our Lord"*. Third, Christ wants to give you God's gift. He wants to enter your life through the gateway of your heart's door. Revelation 3:20 says, *"Behold I stand at the door and knock. If any man hears my voice and opens the door, I will come in unto him and fellowship with him and he with me."* That is God's offer. Jesus is knocking on your heart's door. The question is will you invite him in? Fourth, in order to accept Christ, Romans 10:9, 10 tell us to *"believe in your heart that God has raised him from the dead and you will be saved"*. If you believe that Christ died to pay the penalty for your sin with your whole heart, and that God raised Him from the dead, the Bible declares that you are in right with God, that you are saved, and that heaven is your home.

One of the great benefits of salvation is found in 1 John 1:9 where it says, *"If we confess our sins, He is faithful and just to forgive us our sin and cleanse us from all unrighteousness."* Nothing feels better than to cleansed from our sins. If you have made that decision today, please share it with another Christian. Also, find a good Bible believing church where you can belong so you can grow in your new life. If you would like more information about your new relationship with Jesus Christ, you may contact the author at *melmore6@comcast.net.*

STUDY QUESTIONS

BIBLICAL PERSPECTIVES ON THE CHANGING FACE OF SPIRITUALITY IN MEDICINE

1. Who is the source of all healing and why is this claim made?

2. Where can God's Healing Covenant be found in the Old Testament? What name does God use to identify Himself as our healer?

3. What two New Testament doctrines promise believers access to the healing power of God?

4. What does the Greek Word *sozo* mean? What does the illustration of "the car loan" help understand about healing?

5. History is filled with examples of God's healing. Have you or someone else close to you been healed? Have you seen others healed?

6. Laying On of Hands is a key Biblical teaching regarding healing. Why is it particularly important to understanding touch therapies?

7. List some of the dangers of Reiki, Therapeutic Touch, and Healing Touch?

8. What fundamental biblical doctrines do touch therapies deny?

EPILOGUE

After reading this book you have come to a new awareness of the spiritual backgrounds of certain alternative therapies that are contradictory to your faith in Christ. You may feel surprised and disturbed by the things you have read and rightly so. Perhaps you have heard a great deal about Reiki, Therapeutic Touch, and Healing Touch or have even received training in them? Perhaps you are completely unfamiliar with them at all. Whatever the case, these therapies are being used increasingly in our health care culture and you will be confronted with choices about them very soon.

The question that remains is, "As a Christian, how do I respond to the dangers associated with touch therapies?" Please consider some of the following options as possible responses.

Nurses, Physicians and Other Professionals

- Point out to management the medical studies mentioned in this book and other places concerning the inefficacy of touch therapies. It is difficult to argue with medical literature.
- Point to position statements from major medical institutions such as those mentioned in this book that indicate that many large health care systems do not support the use of touch therapies in their treatment plans.
- Point out the spiritual nature of touch therapies and inform management that not only do they contradict your faith, but they cause you to impose a particular belief system on your patients. Refer patients interested in touch therapies to other health care professionals who perform these treatments.
- Find like-minded co-workers willing to support your position and stand together.

Chaplains and Spiritual Counselors

- Inform management of your discomfort in providing touch therapies, and offer to act as a liaison between the patient requesting services and a practitioner in the community.
- Refer patients to other chaplains who have no qualms about providing such services.
- Ask to be dismissed from training sessions regarding touch therapies on the basis that it violates your ministerial code of ethics.
- Ask not to be required to perform alternative therapies because it contradicts the denominational commitment you are required to uphold as a minister in good standing.

Patients and Family Members

- Refuse to accept touch therapy treatments. You do not have to give a reason; you have the right to refuse any medical treatment you choose.
- If medical personnel begin treatment without asking permission, or if they begin doing something you feel uncomfortable with, tell them to stop immediately! If this continues to be a problem, report it to management and your treating physician.
- If your choice is not respected, do not hesitate to move your loved one to another health care facility that will respect your choices.
- Purchase copies of this book to use as a means to educate others about the dangers of touch therapies in our hospitals and hospices.

Pastors, Teachers and Professors

- Consider hosting a seminar with the author to speak on this topic to your class or congregation.
- Preach a series on the dangers of the occult from the standpoint of Christian apologetics.

- Conduct small group studies of this book based on the study guide within.
- Consult with the author to ask questions and learn more through his email address.
- Use this book as required reading for your class.

You and I are not powerless to take a stand against the occult or the dangers associated with touch therapies and alternative medicine. Ephesians 6:11-16 admonishes us to, *"Put on the full armor of God so that you can take your stand against the devil's schemes. Stand firm then, with the belt of truth buckled around your waist, with the breastplate of righteousness in place, and with your feet fitted with the readiness that comes from the gospel of peace. In addition to all this, take up the shield of faith, with which you can extinguish all the flaming arrows of the evil one."* We must always keep in mind that *"Greater is He that is in you, than he that is in the world"* (1 John 4:4).

BIBLIOGRAPHY

Barnett, L. (1996). Reiki Energy Medicine. Rochester, Vermont: Healing Arts Press.

Bauer, B. (2007). Book of Alternative Medicine. New York, New York: Time Inc.

Borang, K. K. (2000). Reiki. London, UK: Thorsons, an imprint of Harper Collins Publishers.

Brent Bauer, M. D. (2002). Alternative Medicine and Your Health. Rochester, MN: Mayo Clinic Health Information.

Duffield, Guy. (1986). Foundations of Pentecostal Theology. Los Angeles, California: L.I.F.E. Bible College.

Honervogt, T. (1998). The Power of Reiki An Ancient Hands-On Healing Technique. New York, New York: An Owl Book Henry Holt and Company.

Hover-Kramer, D. (2002). Healing Touch: A Guidebook for Practitioners. Albany, New York: Delmar: Thompson Learning.

Jackson, C. &. (2002). A Guide to Reiki. London, UK: Claxton Publishing Group.

Jarrell, D. G. (1997). Reiki Plus: Professional Practioner's Manual for Second Degree. Cookeville, Tennessee: Putnam Printing Inc.

Krieger, D. (1987). Living the Therapeutic Touch: Healing as a Lifestyle. Dodd, Mead & Company: New York, New York.

Krieger, D. (2002). Therapeutic Touch As Transpersonal Healing. New York: Lantern Books.

Kunz, D. (1985). Spiritual Healing. Wheaton, IL: Quest Books: The Theosophical Publishing House.

Lambert, M. (2000). Healing energy for mind, body and Spirit An Introduction to Reiki. London, England: Collins & Brown Limited.

Martin, W. (1997). Kingdom of the Cults. Minneapolis, Minnesota: Bethany House.

McKinzie, E. (1998). Healing Reiki Reuniting Mind, Body, and Spirit with Healing Energy. Berkeley, California: Ulysses Press.

Miles, P. (2008). Reiki: A Comprehensive Guide. London, England: The Penguin Group.

Miller, E. (2008). The Christian, Energetic Medicine, New Age Paranoia. Christian Research Journal, 68 -74.

Murray, S. (2003). Reiki The Ultimate Guide. Las Vegas, Nevada: Body & Mind Productions.

Penczak, C. (2004). Magick of Reiki Focused Energy for Healing: Ritual and Spiritual Development. St. Paul, Minnesota: Llewellyn Publications.

Shannon, S. (2001). Handbook of Complementary and Alternative Therapies in Mental Health. San Diego, CA: Academic Press.

Shuffrey, S. L. (2007). Teach Yourself Reiki. London, England: Bookpoint Ltd.

Sullivan, K. (1998). The Healing Power of Touch: The Many Ways Physical Contact Can Cure. Lincolnwood, Illinois: Publications International Ltd.

Waites, B. (1998). Reiki: A Practical Guide. Hod Hasharon, Israel: Astrolog Publishing House.

Webb, M. (1999). Healing Touch. New York: Sterling Publishing Co.

Wuest, K. S. (1973). Wuest's Word Studies From the Greek New Testament. Grand Rapids, Michigan: Wm. B. Eerdmans Publishing Company.

GLOSSARY OF TERMS

Acupuncture
The procedure of inserting and manipulating needles to relieve pain for therapeutic purposes.

Adepts
A Hindu spirit who has attained a specific level of knowledge and skill.

Alternative Medicine
Any therapy used exclusively apart from traditional medicine.

American Holistic Nurses Association
Association of Holistic nurse practitioners focusing on whole person treatments.

Angels
Heavenly beings created by God but viewed as spirit beings in Touch Therapies.

Animism
Spiritual idea that inanimate beings like, trees, animals and geographical locations have spirits.

APC
Association of Professional Chaplains

APCE
Association for Clinical Pastoral Education

Astral Projection
An astral body capable of traveling outside of the physical body.

Atman
Hinduism's definition of the soul.

Atonement
Christian theology for the process of forgiving a transgression or sin.

Attunement
Reiki ceremony used to advance in Degrees or to increase the ability to heal.

Aura/Etheric Body
Multiple halos of colored light surrounding the human body.

Avatars
Multiple Hindu deities, once human, that incarnate on earth.

Ayurveda
A traditional system of medicine originating in India, from the word 'bonesetting'.

Bhagavad Gita
A Hindu Scripture consisting of 700 verses, given by the god Krishna.

Bio-energy
A contemporary name for the energy derived from the Universal Life Force.

Brahman
The Supreme Cosmic Spirit in Hinduism.

Buddha
Spiritual teacher in northeastern India, the name means, "the Enlightened One".

Buddhism
Asian religion from India founded by Siddhartha Gautama, a religion of ethics based on the cycle of death and rebirth.

Centering/Assessment/Unruffling/Intervention
Practices used during Touch Therapy sessions.

Chakras
The existence of seven energy vortices in the human body, a common idea in Eastern religion.

Channeling
A term used to describe to a medium's ability to act as a spiritual conduit for spirits.

Clairaudience
To gain supernatural information or insight through the sense of hearing.

Claircognizance
To have an innate sense of knowing supernatural information or insight.

Clairsentience
To gain supernatural information or insight through touch.

Clairvoyance
To gain supernatural information or insight through the sense of sight.

Complimentary Medicine
Alternative therapies used in conjunction with traditional medicine.

Conventional Medicine
Traditional scientifically based medical practice.

Counterfeit
That which mimics, commits fraud or impersonates the genuine article.

Devachan
Hindu concept of heaven.

Devas
Any spirit associated with Hinduism.

Dharma
The Buddhist concept of "right teaching" or theology.

Distance Healing
Reiki *practice* of healing at a distance.

Efficacy
The capacity for beneficial change.

Electromagnetism
The physics of the electromagnetic field; the empowering force in Therapeutic Touch.

Energy Medicine
Another name for Touch Therapies based on the concept of the Universal Life Energy.

Enlightenment
Also known as Moshka in Buddhism, it means to liberate or set free through reincarnation.

ESP
Extra Sensory Perception, the ability to connect with the paranormal.

Field Theory
From the science of Quantum Physics used to explain how touch therapies are activated.

Healing Touch
Touch therapy established by Janet Mentgen RN

Higher Sense Perception
The ability to "sense" paranormal activity.

Hinduism
The polytheistic belief system of the Indian subcontinent.

Holistic
Having to do with the whole person, body, mind and spirit.

HPNA
Hospice and Palliative Care Nurses Association, accrediting body for hospices.

Interdisciplinary Team
All medical disciplines that create a team to care for a patient.

ISKCON
Contemporary interpretation of Hinduism in the United States.

JACHO
Joint Commission on the Accreditation of Healthcare Organizations.

Jehovah Rapha
Hebrew phrase meaning, "I am the Lord that Healeth Thee".

Kamaloka
Hindu concept of hell an anteroom for the next life cycle.

Karma
Buddhist and Hindu system of "good or bad works" which affects the next phases of the cycle of reincarnation.

Krishnamurti
Son of Annie Besant, who was to be the next "Buddha" of Theosophy.

Kundalini
A form of Yoga derived from the image of the serpent and reproduces the serpent's movements.

Lady of the Lamp
Name given to Florence Nightingale for her work as a nurse in the Crimean War.

Laying on of hands
Christian practice for invoking the Holy Spirit during healing services, baptisms, blessing, and ordination.

Levels of Consciousness
Theory in Therapeutic Touch based on psychology to describe spirit contact.

Mantra
Phrase used in meditation to focus thought to facilitate spiritual transformation.

Marma Points
A form of acupuncture using imaginary points on the body used to connect energy with the Meridian Lines.

Medical Home Theory
Current Medical Theory in popular use.

Medium
An intermediary between the physical and spiritual worlds.

Meridian Lines
A form of acupuncture using imaginary conduits to direct energy throughout the body.\

Modality
Any method of therapy that involves therapeutic treatment.

Moksha
The Buddhist idea of liberation from the body or reincarnation.

Monad
The human spirit in Hinduism.

NCCAM
The National Center for Complimentary and Alternative Medicine.

Nirvana
The Buddhist idea of heaven, Nirvana is not a place but a state of peace of mind or "nothingness", from the Pali word meaning, "blowing out".

Occult
From the Latin meaning hidden, clandestine, or secret knowledge, it can be detected by the presence of any unexplained phenomena.

Pali Canon
Collection and systemization of the sayings of Buddha compiled 400 years following his death.

Pantheism
The belief that "god is all, and all is god", God is seen as the all-encompassing immanent God and that the Universe and God are equivalent.

Parish Nurse
Movement of over 10,000 Christian registered nurses who integrate faith with the practice of nursing usually in the context of the local church.

Polytheism
The belief in or worship of multiple deities of gods and goddesses, the largest example is Hinduism.

Prana
Sanskrit for "the Vital Life Force" or all-pervasive energy of the universe, and means "breath".

Precognition
Also called Future Sight, it refers to acquiring information through the paranormal.

Psychokinesis
The ability of the mind to move objects through the paranormal.

Qi
The active part of any living thing, translate "energy flow".

Quantum Physics
A scientific set of principles used to describe physical reality at the atomic level.

Redemption of the Body
Christian belief in the physical resurrection of the human body at Christ's return.

Reflexology
An alternative medicine that uses massage to apply pressure to the feet to improve health.

Reiki
An alternative therapy in which practitioners direct "healing energy" to the body through their hands, and is also called "palm healing".

Reiki Degrees
Levels of Reiki initiation including novice, intermediary, and master levels.

Reiki Symbols
Symbols received in Mikao Usui's vision used to activate healing and attunements of practitioners.

Reincarnation
The Hindu belief that the essence of an individual survives death only to be reborn.

Religion
Term defined in health care organizations to mean "rituals or beliefs in traditional religious of faith groups".

Sanskrit
The traditional liturgical language of Hinduism.

Séance
An attempt to communicate with spirits through a session or sitting with a medium.

Shiva, Vishnu, Krishna
The Hindu triad or trinity of its chief manifestations in the Hiegharchy of gods.

Shuman Wave
Hertz waves measured at 7-85 Hz Common to all of nature, but used to explain the activating electrical field in Healing Touch.

Siddhartha Gautama
The birth name of Buddha.

Sozo
The Greek word meaning healing, wholeness and salvation.

Spirit Guide
An entity that remains incorporeal to communicate or incarnate through human beings.

Spiritism
French philosophy developed in the mid-nineteenth century that believes in the existence of and communication with spirits.

Spirits
Incorporeal beings of demonic origins, they may manifest as deceased loved ones.

Spirituality
Defined within health care as "seeing the person as a whole being", it sees itself as separate from God, or religious practices and beliefs; much of its focus is on emotional well-being.

Study
An in-depth medical analysis of a particular treatment used to define efficacy.

Subtle Bodies/Energies
The belief in the existence of psycho-spiritual bodies surrounding the physical body, also known as auras.

Sutras
A literary form of Hindu and Buddhist Scriptures used for ease of memorization.

Syncretism
The attempt to reconcile unrelated or contrary beliefs, while melding their practices together.

Talking Boards
Early form of Ouija Boards used in the 19th Century.

Taoism
Meaning, "the path or way", it is a Chinese folk religion emphasizing astrology, martial arts, magic and incantations.

Telepathy
The paranormal transference of thoughts, information, or feelings between individuals.

The Four Nobel Truths
First teachings of Buddha that deal with the nature of suffering.

The Middle Way
Buddhist practice of non-extremism.

Theism
The belief in a single deity, exemplified in Christianity and Judaism.

Theosophical Society
An organization founded in 1875 to advance the spiritual principles of Helena Blavatsky.

Theosophy
The belief that all religions have a portion of the truth and help humanity move on to perfection.

Therapeutic Touch
An energy therapy which claims to reduce pain and anxiety and effect healing through touch.

Three Declared Objects
The foundational doctrines of Theosophy.

Traditional Chinese Medicine
Philosophy derived from Taoist and Buddhist thought and includes many practices including acupuncture, herbal medicine, Shiatsu massage, the chakra and meridian system.

Universal Life Force
Energy fields which surround the entire earth, based on Buddhist pantheistic ideas and describes them as a spiritual power.

Upanishads
The oldest of Hindu religious literature and constitute its core teaching.

Vedas
Ancient Hindu Scriptures contain hymns, magical formulas, chants and history.

Vital Life Force
The Hindu version of the energy fields (prana) which surround the earth and from which emanates a spiritual healing power.

Yin and Yang
Buddhist philosophy used to describe how opposing forces are actually interconnected.

Yoga
Consisting of various branches, yoga is a physical and mental discipline and is the highest method of Hindu worship.

ABOUT THE AUTHOR

Michael Elmore holds a Doctoral degree from Ashland Theological Seminary. He is also the editor of several textbooks used around the globe by Bible Colleges and seminaries to train ministers. Dr. Elmore wrote a Christian-based weekly newspaper column for a number of years and contributed to Cecil Murphey's exciting book, "I Believe in Heaven."

As a pastor for over three decades, Dr. Elmore has served throughout the Midwest in both rural and urban communities. Dr. Elmore worked as a chaplain for over 16 years at two community hospitals, a large state tertiary hospital, and later as a chaplain for a freestanding hospice house and community-based hospice programs. He has also been involved in prison ministry and appeared on television and radio.

Dr. Elmore and his wife Coleen have been married for over 44 years and have three children. Jessica, Jennifer, and Andrew. The couple also has seven grandchildren: Aaron, Alex, Billie, Natalie, Benjamin, Adalynn, and Aiden. All of them are bright, healthy, and have lots of fun.

SUBJECT INDEX

www.ingramcontent.com/pod-product-compliance
Lightning Source LLC
Chambersburg PA
CBHW070919120626
46546CB00001B/328